THE WORDSWORTHS AND THE LAKES

Home at
Grasmere

THE WORDSWORTHS AND THE LAKES

HOME AT GRASMERE

Penelope Hughes-Hallett

C&B

COLLINS & BROWN

First published in Great Britain in 1993
by Collins & Brown Limited
Mercury House
195 Knightsbridge
London SW7 1RE

Conceived, edited and designed by Collins & Brown Limited

Editor: Elizabeth Drury
Picture Research: Philippa Lewis
Art Director: Roger Bristow
Styled by: Ruth Hope
Designed by: Bill Mason

Typeset by Goodfellow & Egan, Cambridge
Reproduction by J Film, Bangkok
Printed and bound in Italy by New Interlitho SpA

CONTENTS

INTRODUCTION

SOON AFTER reaching Grasmere in Christmas week 1799 the young William Wordsworth expressed his feelings of joy in the poem 'Home at Grasmere', taken as the title of this book. At Dove Cottage he and his sister Dorothy settled together into their small home, to them a paradise after years of separation from each other and of exile from the Lakes. 'Home' implied a return to their roots, to the countryside of their birth. Here William was to compose the major body of his work. Surrounded by the lakes and valleys of his childhood, and cherished and encouraged by his beloved Dorothy, he could pursue that life of the imagination, the key to spiritual awareness, in which state, he said, 'We see into the life of things.'

Although solitude was always precious to William and Dorothy, they did not live the lives of hermits. They became, rather, the centre of an ardent and loving circle that included Thomas De Quincey, Robert Southey and, pre-eminently, Samuel Taylor Coleridge. William married Mary Hutchinson in 1802 and in the following years they had five children. Sara, Mary's sister and the adored of Coleridge, also joined the Wordsworth household. This little company of extraordinarily gifted men and women lived their lives with an eager intensity, whether they were loving, quarrelling, laughing, mourning or striding over enormous tracts of mountainous country, glorying as they went in the beauties of the Lakes about which they felt so proprietorial.

Above all, they wrote and wrote: poems, diaries, notebooks and long letters. As their fame grew, others outside their charmed circle wrote about them too. The happy result for posterity is that they can tell their own story, speaking directly and spontaneously to the reader of today. And so, in this book, which is an account of the daily life of the Wordsworths and

LEFT *Wordsworth, describing the effects of 'skiey influences' on the Lakes, wrote of 'fleecy clouds resting upon the hill tops; they are not easily managed in picture, with their accompaniments of blue sky; but how glorious they are in Nature! how pregnant with imagination for the poet! and the height of the Cumbrian mountains is sufficient to exhibit daily and hourly instances of those mysterious attachments.'*
A study of cumulus clouds by John Constable, 1822.

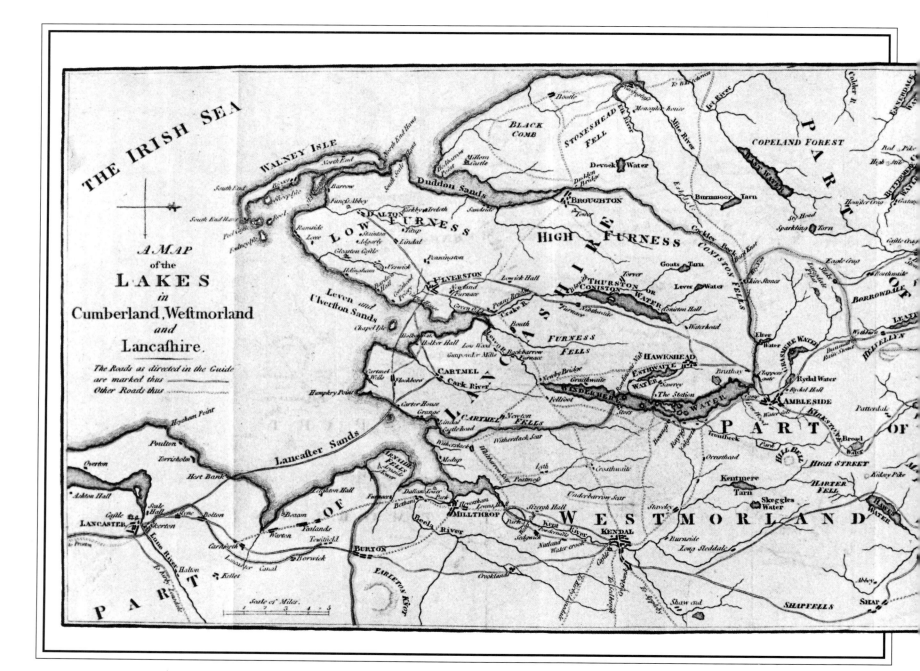

their friends in the first years of the nineteenth century, their own voices predominate. Life was full of extremes of ecstasy and grief; but all the while there was also a steady flow of mundane happenings, vivid in their simplicity. We hear of Coleridge in bed eating a mutton chop; Wordsworth sitting at breakfast in his open shirt, neglecting his basin of broth and writing a poem to a butterfly; Dorothy making a mattress or copying out her brother's nearly indecipherable verse. In this way of life, with its combination of the visionary and the everyday, William could achieve the sought-after harmony with the natural world that formed the bedrock of his poetry. No other landscape provided so potent an inspiration for his imagination as did these lakes and hills, hallowed by the memory of his childhood dreams, so that he could feel

> *A presence that disturbs me with the joy*
> *Of elevated thoughts; a sense sublime*
> *Of something far more deeply interfused,*
> *Whose dwelling is the light of setting suns,*
> *And the round ocean and the living air,*
> *And the blue sky, and in the mind of man;*

The works that emerged from this fortunate confluence of poetic genius and natural beauty have become a part of the furniture of all our minds.

LEFT *Map of the Lakes. William Wordsworth spent most of his life within these boundaries. In 'Home at Grasmere' he wrote exultantly: 'Embrace me, then, ye Hills, and close me in, / Now in the clear and open day I feel / Your guardianship. I take it to my heart; / 'Tis like the solemn shelter of the night.'*

𝒫RELUDE
TO THE 𝓛AKES

RIGHT *View in Borrowdale, a watercolour by Rev. Joseph Wilkinson. William's poems and Dorothy's journal are full of references to scenery such as this. 'William observed some affecting little things in Borrowdale,' wrote Dorothy. 'A decayed house . . . in the churchyard, the tall silent rocks seen through the broken windows. A kind of rough column put upon the gavel end of a house with a ball stone smooth from the river placed upon it for ornament. Near it one stone like it upon an old mansion carefully hewn.'*

AT HALF PAST FOUR in the afternoon of 21 December 1799 William and Dorothy Wordsworth crossed the threshold of Dove Cottage at Town End, Grasmere. Brother and sister were exhausted, dirty and cold after their three days' journey from Yorkshire, much of it made on foot. But both were also alight with exultation, being about to realize their cherished dream of returning to live together in the Lake country of their childhood memories, and, best of all, to be in Grasmere, where William had vowed as a boy that 'here / Should be my home, this Valley be my World'. 'And now,' he could triumphantly add, ''tis mine for life; dear Vale, / One of thy lowly dwellings is my home!'

William and Dorothy had been born within a year of one another—in 1770 and 1771. They and their three brothers spent a happy, untrammelled childhood, living in a handsome eighteenth-century house looking over the River Derwent—William's 'fairest of all rivers'—at Cockermouth in Cumberland. Their father John was legal and political agent to the powerful Sir James Lowther, created first Earl of Lonsdale in 1794; their mother Ann was the daughter of a prosperous linen draper in Penrith.

In his autobiographical poem *The Prelude* William recalled those carefree years among the lakes and mountains:

> *Oh, many a time have I, a five years' child,*
> *In a small mill-race severed from his stream,*
> *Made one long bathing of a summer's day;*
> *Basked in the sun, and plunged and basked again*
> *Alternate, all a summer's day, or scoured*

The sandy fields, leaping through flowery groves
Of yellow ragwort; or when rock and hill,
The woods, and distant Skiddaw's lofty height,
Were bronzed with deepest radiance, stood alone
Beneath the sky, as if I had been born
On Indian plains, and from my mother's hut
Had run abroad in wantonness, to sport,
A naked savage, in the thunder shower.

From the very first William and Dorothy were boon companions, and Dorothy's intuitive qualities, even at a tender age, were gratefully remembered by her brother:

The Blessing of my later years
Was with me when a Boy:
She gave me eyes, she gave me ears;
And humble cares, and delicate fears;
A heart, the fountain of sweet tears;
And love, and thought, and joy.

When William was eight his mother died and Dorothy was sent away to live with cousins at Halifax in Yorkshire. She was kindly treated, but the separation from her brothers, especially from William, left her for the rest of her life with a passionate, almost obsessive, love of family. And then, in 1783, Mr Wordsworth died, leaving his children almost penniless, largely owing to an unpaid debt of Lord Lonsdale, the cause of much trouble in the following years.

As a schoolboy in the Lakes William enjoyed skating, boating and bird's-nesting as much as did his fellows. But from the beginning strange presences seemed to surround him, and he would fall into trance-like states when he 'grasped at a wall or tree to recall myself from this abyss of idealism to the reality'.

One evening he found a shepherd's boat moored to a willow tree and took it out on the lake:

LEFT *Wordsworth's birthplace, Cockermouth, the poet's home for the first nine years of his life. On the banks of the Derwent, the sound of the river formed the background to his childhood. 'Fair seed-time had my soul,' he declared in* The Prelude, *'and I grew up / Fostered alike by beauty and by fear; / Much favoured in my birthplace.'*

> *It was an act of stealth*
> *And troubled pleasure . . . .*
> *I dipped my oars into the silent lake,*
> *And, as I rose upon the stroke, my boat*
> *Went heaving through the water like a swan;*
> *When, from behind that craggy steep till then*
> *The horizon's bound, a huge peak, black and huge,*
> *As if with voluntary power instinct*
> *Upreared its head. I struck and struck again,*
> *And growing still in stature the grim shape*
> *Towered up between me and the stars, and still,*
> *For so it seemed, with purpose of its own*
> *And measured motion like a living thing,*
> *Strode after me. With trembling oars I turned,*
> *And through the silent water stole my way*
> *Back to the covert of the willow tree;*
> *There in her mooring-place I left my bark, —*
> *And through the meadows homeward went, in grave*
> *And serious mood.*

For days after the boy was oppressed by an enveloping dark-ness, 'call it solitude / Or blank desertion', in which state nothing of the familiar landscape remained

> But huge and mighty forms, that do not live
> Like living men, moved slowly through the mind
> By day, and were a trouble to my dreams.

At night he heard 'low breathings' coming after him:

>   oh, at that time
> While on the perilous ridge I hung alone,
> With what strange utterance did the loud dry wind
> Blow through my ear! the sky seemed not a sky
> Of earth—and with what motion moved the clouds!

In 1787 William left Hawkshead Grammar School and spent his holidays at Penrith, where Dorothy was by then living with her Cookson grandparents, unhappy except in the companionship of another orphan, Mary Hutchinson, destined to be her lifelong friend. The three young people passed happy weeks tramping over and among the Cumberland hills.

Rumblings from the Revolution in France formed the back-drop to William's youth. It was during his second visit to France, in 1791, that a libertarian fervour took hold of his imagination. Society was in a state of flux; dangers proliferated; but for the young and ardent life was intoxicating. Looking back on this early time, William was memorably to exclaim:

> Bliss was it in that dawn to be alive,
> But to be young was very Heaven!

The heady concepts of freedom, revolt and of the equality of men now inflamed his emotions, already in a highly exalted state from his love affair with Annette Vallon, the daughter of a

ABOVE *Miniature, a presumed portrait of Annette Vallon, with whom Wordsworth fell in love in revolutionary France in 1791. Their child, Caroline, was born a year later, but the hostilities between England and France separated the lovers, and Wordsworth did not meet his daughter until she was nine.*

surgeon at Blois, whom he met at Orléans and who bore him a child. Before the birth William returned to London, probably to raise funds; but the increasing stranglehold of the Terror and France's declaration of war precluded an immediate return to Blois. Earlier he had written urgently for help to his brother Richard, ending 'Adieu, Adieu, you will send the money immediately.' A few poignant letters from Annette have survived, showing that she described herself as William's wife and expected that he would marry her. In one, written to Dorothy, she said:

> Often when I am alone in my room with his letters, I dream he is going to walk in. I stand ready to throw myself into his arms and say to him: 'Come my love, come and dry these tears which have long been flowing for you, let us fly and see Caroline, our child and your likeness.'

But it was not until his daughter was nine years old that William was to meet her or to see her mother again.

In 1795 William and Dorothy were reunited. Dorothy had spent the previous years with her uncle, the parson William Cookson, and his wife in Norfolk, helping to look after their four children and carrying out the usual domestic duties of the unmarried poor relation. She had to endure 'a painful idea that one's existence is of very little use which *I* really have always been obliged to feel'; and in her heart she dreamed of a future in which she and William might set up house on their own account. Her brother had been passing through a period of anguish, oppressed by the trauma of his separation from Annette and the horrors of the regime in France, uncertain as to the future direction of his life, but always convinced of his vocation as poet, which he had come to see as an inner revolution, not of violence but of attitude. If man could live in harmony with himself and with nature, he argued, then harmony with his fellow men must surely follow; hence his poetic gift should

LEFT *Penrith. Dorothy lived here for a while, homesick and lonely, with her Cookson grandparents. The one saving grace of this time was her friendship with another orphan, Mary Hutchinson, destined to play a central role in the Wordsworths' lives.*

be directed towards the realization of this unifying moral vision. He had become conscious of his destiny, he related in *The Prelude*, on walking home after a night of 'dancing gaiety and mirth' in the Lakes, when he saw the dawn break in such magnificence

> *that to the brim*
> *My heart was full; I made no vows, but vows*
> *Were then made for me; bond unknown to me*
> *Was given, that I should be, else sinning greatly,*
> *A dedicated Spirit.*

A princely and unexpected legacy of £900 came to William in 1795 from a school friend, Raisley Calvert, who, convinced of his genius, had hoped the bequest might protect the poet from the distractions of earning his living by other, more mundane, means. In the same year he was lent a Dorset farmhouse, Racedown, where he was joined by Dorothy. Soothed and encouraged by her, he gradually found himself able to write:

> *She, in the midst of all, preserved me still*
> *A Poet, made me seek beneath that name,*
> *And that alone, my office upon earth:*

In March 1797 Dorothy wrote to Jane Marshall, who as Jane Pollard had been her childhood companion in Halifax days: 'You perhaps have heard that my friend Mary Hutchinson is staying with me; she is one of the best girls in the world and we are as happy as human beings can be; that is when William is at home . . . he is the life of the whole house.'

Their next visitor was Samuel Taylor Coleridge. Coleridge, youngest of the nine sons of the vicar of Ottery St Mary, had been something of a child prodigy. His mercurial temperament and occasional violent rages alienated him from his brothers and the result was a lonely childhood. On his father's death he

ABOVE *Profile drawing of Charles Lamb in 1798, a year after his visit to Coleridge at Nether Stowey and his meeting with the Wordsworths. Lamb, an erudite and gentle humorist, is best remembered for his* Essays of Elia *and, with his sister Mary,* Tales from Shakespeare.

was sent to Christ's Hospital school in London, where his intellectual prowess and the brilliance and range of his talk brought him schoolboy fame and the admiration of such fellow students as Charles Lamb.

At Cambridge, despite flashes of academic achievement presaging his formidable powers as thinker and poet, he behaved with a flamboyant excess that led to illness and debt. In despair he enlisted in the 15th Light Dragoons under the name of Silas Tomkyn Comberbache, a predicament from which he was retrieved by his brother George, on a plea of insanity.

With a young radical poet, Robert Southey, Coleridge planned the setting up of a commune on the banks of the Susquehanna river in New England, where twelve men and twelve young women would, they hoped, live out an egalitarian idyll. This scheme, known to the poets as 'Pantisocracy', never materialized, its one lasting consequence being the marriage between Coleridge and Southey's sister-in-law, Sara Fricker, a milliner, disastrously undertaken by Coleridge in response to pressures from Southey. Initially the pair were happy enough and, after the birth of their first child, Hartley, they moved to a cottage at Nether Stowey in Somerset, where Coleridge struggled to support his little family by means of journalism and poetry. He gave a wry description of himself at this time to John Thelwall, the revolutionary political lecturer:

My face, unless when animated by immediate eloquence, expresses great sloth, and great, indeed, almost idiotic good-nature. 'T is a mere carcass of a face . . . As to my shape, 't is a good shape enough if measured, but my gait is awkward, and the walk of the whole man indicates *indolence capable of energies*. I am, and ever have been, a great reader, and have read almost everything—a library cormorant. I am *deep* in all out of the way books, whether of the monkish times, or of the puritanical era. I have read and digested most of the historical writers; but I do not *like* history. Metaphysics and poetry and

ABOVE *Portrait of Coleridge.'He is pale and thin,' wrote Dorothy, 'has a wide mouth, thick lips, and not very good teeth, longish loose-growing half-curling rough black hair. But if you hear him speak for five minutes you think no more of them. His eye is large and full, not dark but grey; such an eye as would receive from a heavy soul the dullest expression; but it speaks every emotion of his animated mind; it has more of the "poet's eye in a fine frenzy rolling" than I ever witnessed.'*

'facts of mind,' that is, accounts of all the strange phantasms that ever possessed 'your philosophy;' dreamers, from Thoth the Egyptian to Taylor the English pagan, are my darling studies. In short, I seldom read except to amuse myself, and I am almost always reading. Of useful knowledge, I am a so-so chemist, and I love chemistry. All else is *blank;* but I *will* be (please God) an horticulturalist and a farmer. I compose very little, and I absolutely hate composition, and such is my dislike that even a sense of duty is sometimes too weak to overpower it.

I cannot breathe through my nose, so my mouth, with sensual thick lips, is almost always open. In conversation I am impassioned, and oppose what I deem error with an eagerness which is often mistaken for personal asperity; but I am ever so swallowed up in the *thing* that I *perfectly* forget my *opponent.*

ABOVE *Drawing by S. L. May of Racedown, Dorset. This is the farmhouse where, thanks to a legacy from his friend Raisley Calvert, William was able to make a home in 1795 with Dorothy and where, encouraged by his sister, he settled to writing poetry.*

William later remembered Coleridge's first arrival at Racedown: 'He did not keep to the high road, but leaped over a gate and bounded down a pathless field, by which he cut off an angle', a wonderfully typical entrance, Coleridge literally flying through the air into the Wordsworths' lives. He, for his part, wrote to his Bristol publisher:

Wordsworth and his exquisite Sister are with me—She is a woman indeed!—in mind, I mean, and heart—for her person is such, that if you expected to see a pretty woman, you would think her ordinary—if you expected to find an ordinary woman, you would think her pretty!—But her manners are simple, ardent, impressive . . . Her information various—her eye watchful in minutest observation of nature—and her taste a perfect electrometer—it bends, protrudes, and draws in, at subtlest beauties and most recondite faults.

And to Southey he described Wordsworth as 'a very great man—the only man, to whom at all times and in all modes of excellence I feel myself inferior.'

RIGHT *Alfoxden Park, Somerset, by Coplestone Warre Bamfylde. The young Wordsworths moved to Alfoxden (for which they paid a peppercorn rent) in order to be nearer to Coleridge at Nether Stowey. Dorothy described it as 'a large mansion in a large park, with seventy head of deer around us'. She and William do not seem to have been unduly overwhelmed by the splendour.*

The Wordsworths soon moved to be closer to Coleridge, taking Alfoxden, a large house near Nether Stowey, at a nominal rent. Here they met Coleridge's wife Sara and baby Hartley; and also the essayist Charles Lamb, still distraught from the shock of coming upon his sister Mary, knife in hand, having just killed their mother in a fit of madness. In his strange poem 'Old Familiar Faces' Lamb wrote of this horror:

> *Where are they gone, the old familiar faces?*
> *I had a mother, but she died and left me,*
> *Died prematurely in a day of horrors—*
> *All, all, are gone, the old familiar faces.*

His visit was the occasion of Coleridge's 'This Lime-Tree Bower my Prison'. In a letter to Southey of 17 July 1797 Coleridge explained how the poem came to be written:

Charles Lamb has been with me for a week. He left me Friday morning. The second day after Wordsworth came to me, dear Sara accidentally emptied a skillet of boiling milk on my foot, which confined me during the whole time of C. Lamb's stay and still prevents me from all *walks* longer than a furlong. While Wordsworth, his sister, and Charles Lamb were out one evening, sitting in the arbour of T. Poole's garden which communicates with mine, I wrote these lines, with which I am pleased.

The poem began:

Well, they are gone, and here I must remain,
This lime-tree bower my prison.

The poet pictured to himself the progress of his friends in their long rambles and ended the poem on a quiet note with the coming of night. The lovely meditation was addressed to Lamb, who resented being apostrophized as 'gentle-hearted Charles', although his nature was indeed a gentle one as his devoted care of his adored Mary amply showed. Her recurrent fits of madness desolated him and there is a sad account of brother and sister setting off resolutely together to the madhouse, Charles carrying Mary's strait-jacket.

During the next year of felicitous collaboration with Coleridge, Wordsworth wrote all the poems comprising his share in *Lyrical Ballads*, ending with the magisterially beautiful 'Lines Composed a few Miles above Tintern Abbey'. Coleridge contributed 'The Rime of the Ancient Mariner' and had begun the first part of 'Christabel'.

The Alfoxden period was for the Wordsworths and Coleridge a time of excitement, of long, long walks, often by night, discussing philosophy, poetry, love and life. The threesome's odd habits, eccentric appearance and passionate declamation of verse led to suspicions of their being Jacobin spies; no light

RIGHT *Tintern Abbey. Wordsworth contributed 'Lines Composed a few Miles above Tintern Abbey' to* Lyrical Ballads, *published in 1798.*

matter while England felt herself threatened by invasion from France. William Hazlitt, the essayist and critic, described William's manner at this time:

> The next day Wordsworth arrived from Bristol at Coleridge's cottage . . . He was quaintly dressed . . . in a brown fustian jacket and striped pantaloons . . . There was a severe, worn pressure of thought about his temples, a fire in his eye (as if he saw something in objects more than the outward appearance), an intense high narrow forehead, a Roman nose . . . and a convulsive inclination to laughter about the mouth . . . He sat down and talked very naturally and freely, with a mixture of clear gushing accents in his voice, a deep guttural intonation, and a strong tincture of the northern *burr*, like the crust on wine. He instantly began to make havoc of the half of a Cheshire cheese on the table.

Wordsworth would, for example, have pronounced 'waters' to rhyme with 'chatters'; Coleridge, for his part, spoke with a strong West Country accent.

Hazlitt went on to describe the characteristic differences between the two poets' manners of composition and declamation:

> There is a *chaunt* in the recitation both of Coleridge and Wordsworth, which acts as a spell upon the hearer, and disarms the judgment . . . Coleridge's manner is more full, animated, and varied; Wordsworth's more equable, sustained, and internal. The one might be termed more *dramatic*, the other more *lyrical*. Coleridge has told me that he himself liked to compose in walking over uneven ground, or breaking through the straggling branches of a copse-wood; whereas Wordsworth always wrote (if he could) walking up and down a straight gravel-walk, or in some spot where the continuity of his verse met with no collateral interruption.

ABOVE *Wordsworth as a young man in 1798 drawn by Robert Hancock. Hazlitt described the poet at that time as having a 'severe, worn pressure of thought about his temple, a fire in his eye . . . and a convulsive inclination to laughter about the mouth'. His voice was 'a mixture of clear gushing accents . . . and a strong tincture of the northern* burr, *like the crust on wine'.*

His account evokes that time of exhilaration and happiness better than any other has done:

> Returning that same evening, I got into a metaphysical argument with Wordsworth, while Coleridge was explaining the different notes of the nightingale to his sister, in which we neither of us succeeded in making ourselves perfectly clear and intelligible. Thus I passed three weeks at Nether Stowey and in the neighbourhood, generally devoting the afternoons to a delightful chat in an arbour made of bark by the poet's friend Tom Poole, sitting under two fine elm-trees, and listening to the bees humming round us, while we quaffed our *flip*.

Coleridge, writing to the political philosopher William Godwin of his relationship with the Wordsworths, exclaimed half-jokingly, 'though we were three persons it was but one God.' Certainly the intensity of their happy rapport resulted in much glorious verse. 'The Ancient Mariner', for example, evolved during a prolonged tour of the Somerset hills, with William contributing ideas (one of these being the death of the albatross) and Dorothy's lightning perceptions providing the extra stimulus that spurred the two poets on to further achievement.

The figure of Sara Coleridge was notably absent from all this heady exaltation. She and Coleridge still enjoyed harmonious interludes together, but decreasingly so, and her husband was already beginning to find her company a duty rather than a source of joy.

In 1798 the Alfoxden lease expired and the Wordsworths, with Coleridge, spent some months in Germany, Sara being left behind with her baby. On their return to England, William and Dorothy travelled north to stay with the Hutchinson family in Northumberland, near Sockburn on Tees, where Mary, with her sisters Sara and Joanna, kept house for their brothers. Coleridge arrived at Sockburn in the autumn of 1799 and he and William set off together for a tour of the Lakes, where by

RIGHT *Rydal Water, 'taken at the Going of a Storm', signed by Francis Towne and dated 1786. At a later recurrence of such raking light over the lake Wordsworth watched as a mirage-like effect was created, so that the mountains seemed to rise like Jacob's Ladder into the sky: 'Wings at my shoulder seem to play; / But, rooted here, I stand and gaze / On those bright steps that heavenward raise / Their practicable way.'*

happy chance they encountered John Wordsworth, William's sailor brother, who joined their party. Together the poets wrote to Dorothy, their letter overflowing with enjoyment and mooting for the first time the possibility of a home in the Lakes.

> C. was much struck with Grasmere and its neighbourhood and I have much to say to you, you will think my plan a mad one, but I have thought of building a house there by the Lake side. John would give me £40 to buy the ground, and for £250 I am sure I could build one as good as we can wish . . . I think it will be ten days before we shall see you. There is a small house at Grasmere empty which perhaps we may take, and purchase furniture but of this we will speak. But I shall write again when I know more on this subject.

Coleridge added his enthusiasm:

> You can feel what I cannot express for myself—how deeply I have been impressed by a world of scenery absolutely new to me. At Rydal and Grasmere I recd I think the deepest delight, yet Hawes Water thro' many a varying view kept my eyes dim with tears, and this evening, approaching Derwentwater in diversity of harmonious features, in the majesty of its beauties and in the Beauty of its majesty—O my God! . . . It was to me a vision of a fair Country. Why were you not with us Dorothy? Why were not you Mary with us?

Later, back at Sockburn, the beginning of Coleridge's doomed passion for Sara Hutchinson was confided to his notebooks: 'Nov 24th—the Sunday—Conundrums and Puns and Stories and Laughter—with Jack Hutchinson—Stood round the Fire.' Coleridge then broke into Latin, which has been translated as 'and I held Sara's hand for a long time behind my back, and then for the first time, Love pierced me with its dart, envenomed, and alas! incurable!'

ABOVE *Snow-capped mountains from a sketchbook by John Glover. Dorothy wrote: 'the mountains of Easedale, black or covered with snow at the tops, gave a peculiar softness to the valley. The clouds hid the tops of some of them.'*

It was probably at Sockburn during this visit, and with his mind full of Sara, or 'Asra' as he wrote of her in a transposition of her name, that Coleridge composed his poem 'Love'.

All thoughts, all passions, all delights,
Whatever stirs this mortal frame,
All are but ministers of Love,
*   And feed his sacred flame.*

Sara Hutchinson was at this time twenty-four years old. By all accounts she was no beauty, scarcely more than five feet tall, with homely features and a determined jaw. But she was also the possessor of a glowing skin and a mass of light brown hair (or auburn—opinions vary); and she was neat and quick in her movements. Much of her attraction for Coleridge lay in her ready sympathy, her immediate response to beauty, whether in nature or in poetry, and her instinctive understanding of his mind and mercurial temperament.

If they had been free to marry, the whole course of Coleridge's life might have been different. Their tragedy was that they did not meet until five years after his marriage to Sara Fricker. His religious scruples on the sanctity of that bond locked him in a relationship in which the temperamental gap between husband and wife was too wide to bridge, while Sara Coleridge's complaints and jealousies led increasingly to bitter misunderstandings.

In sharp contrast, for the Wordsworths this was a time of joy; of long-held dreams about to be realized of settling together in the Lakes. The decision to move north was taken and, during the course of their long and hard winter journey, a strange visionary trance at Hartleap Well, experienced by both, and later described by William, seemed to confirm them in the rightness of their enterprise and filled them with a sense of elation that carried them on towards their goal. Ahead lay Dove Cottage and the Grasmere years.

ABOVE *Pencil drawing of Dorothy Wordsworth. Coleridge was struck by her expressive features and 'her eye watchful in minutest observation of nature'. Thomas De Quincey also remarked on the compelling quality of her gaze.*

DOVE COTTAGE

$\mathscr{A}$RRIVAL AT $\mathscr{G}$RASMERE

RIGHT *Grasmere Lake, a coloured print by John La Porte. Wordsworth's deep love for Grasmere stemmed from the sense it gave him: 'Of majesty and beauty and repose, / A blended holiness of earth and sky, / Something that makes this individual spot . . . / Perfect contentment, unity entire.'*

THE VALE OF GRASMERE, as the Wordsworths saw it at the turn of the eighteenth century, must have appeared a veritable Elysium. A few years later Thomas De Quincey gave a bird's-eye view description of it, looking down from Coniston:

> The whole vale of Grasmere suddenly breaks upon the view in a style of almost theatrical surprise, with its lovely valley stretching in the distance, the lake lying immediately below, with its solemn bent-like island of five acres in size, seemingly floating on its surface; its exquisite outline on the opposite shore, revealing all its little bays and wild sylvan margin, feathered to the edge with wild flowers and ferns . . . a few green fields; and beyond them, just two bowshots from the water, a little white cottage gleaming from the midst of trees, with a vast and seemingly never-ending series of ascents, rising above it to the height of more than three thousand feet. That little cottage was Wordsworth's.

Here, William determined, he would pursue his poetic vocation, which he fervently believed would help to bring mankind to a higher state of moral awareness. He saw the poet, as he would later write in a celebrated phrase, as 'the rock of defence of human nature; an upholder and preserver, carrying every where with him relationship and love'.

For the immediate present William and Dorothy's task was to make themselves a home. Old Molly Fisher, their neighbour from across the road, had been engaged to light the fire against

their arrival, but achieved only a thin glow of dying embers. Years later she reminded Dorothy of that first meeting: 'I mun never forget 't laal striped gown and 't laal straw bonnet as ye stood there.'

The cottage consisted of only two downstairs rooms and a back kitchen, with four tiny rooms above. Here the Wordsworths settled to a multiplicity of tasks, William giving his first impressions of these in a Christmas Eve letter to Coleridge in something of the tone of a child, ecstatic with a new toy, who tries not to boast its possession:

My dearest Coleridge

We arrived here last Friday, and have now been four days in our new abode without writing to you, a long time! but we have been in such confusion as not to have had a moment's leisure . . . D is now sitting by me racked with the tooth-ache. This is a grievous misfortune as she has so much work for her needle among the bedcurtains etc. that she is absolutely buried in it. We have both caught troublesome colds in our new and almost empty house, but we hope to make it a comfortable dwelling . . . We have agreed to give a woman who lives in one of the adjoining cottages two shillings a week for attending two or three hours a day to light the fires wash dishes etc. . . . We could have had this attendance for eighteen pence a week but we added the sixpence for the sake of the poor woman, who is made happy by it.

Wordsworth concluded his letter with what was to become a familiar complaint:

Composition I find invariably pernicious to me, and even penmanship if continued for any length of time at one sitting. I shall therefore wish you good night, my beloved friend, a wish, with a thousand others, in which D joins me. I am afraid half of what I have written is illegible, farewell.

RIGHT *Dove Cottage, a watercolour by Amos Green. Originally an inn, the Olive-bough and Dove, it was always referred to by the Wordsworths as Town End, 'our beautiful and quiet home', as William called it. He wrote to Coleridge on their first arrival that: 'D. is much pleased with the house and* appurtenances, *the orchard especially; in imagination she has already built a seat with a summer shed on the highest platform of this our little domestic slip of mountain.'*

Somewhat typically, Wordsworth had found time, as he wrote to Coleridge, to borrow skates, while Dorothy continued to work. In his mind (as would have been plain to Coleridge from the phrases 'clear as polished steel' and 'give my body to the wind' in his friend's letter) was the skating sequence in *The Prelude*, written during the previous bitter winter in Germany:

> *All shod with steel,*
> *We hissed along the polished ice in games*
> *Confederate, imitative of the chase*
> *And woodland pleasures, – the resounding horn,*
> *The pack loud chiming, and the hunted hare.*
> *So through the darkness and the cold we flew,*
> *And not a voice was idle; with the din*
> *Smitten, the precipices rang aloud;*

The leafless trees and every icy crag
Tinkled like iron; while far distant hills
Into the tumult sent an alien sound
Of melancholy not unnoticed, while the stars
Eastward were sparkling clear, and in the west
The orange sky of evening died away.

One of William and Dorothy's first tasks was the creation of a garden. 'We mean,' Wordsworth explained to Coleridge,

> to enclose two or three yards of ground between us and the road, this for the sake of a few flowers, and because it will make it more our own. Besides, am I fanciful when I would extend the obligation of gratitude to insensate things? May not a man have a salutary pleasure in doing something gratuitously for the sake of his house, as for an individual to which he owes so much.

And Dorothy, to her friend Jane Marshall, continued the account:

> We have a boat upon the lake and a small orchard and a smaller *garden* which as it is the work of our own hands we regard with pride and partiality . . . Our cottage is quite large enough for us though very small, and we have made it neat and comfortable within doors, and it looks very nice on the outside, for though the roses and honeysuckles which we have planted against it are only of this year's growth yet it is covered all over with green leaves and scarlet flowers, for we have trained scarlet beans upon threads, which are not only exceedingly beautiful, but very useful, as their produce is immense . . . We have made a lodging room of the parlour below stairs, which has a stone floor, therefore we have covered it all over with matting. The bed, though only a camp bed, is large enough for two people to sleep in. We sit in a

LEFT *Sailing on Loweswater, an early nineteenth-century print. William and Dorothy owned a boat such as these, from which they fished—on one occasion Dorothy recorded a catch of thirteen bass—or sometimes just drifted, reciting or reading aloud. Dorothy wrote, in July 1800, of an occasion when Coleridge was with them: 'Read poems on the water and let the boat take its own course. We walked a long time on Loughrigg and returned in the grey twilight.'*

BELOW *Dorothy wrote to her friend Jane Marshall boasting of the beauties of the Dove Cottage garden and of the young honeysuckle and roses she was training against the cottage walls. She noticed wild roses beginning to bloom, but added: 'I have seen no honeysuckles yet except our own one nestling.'*

room above stairs and we have one lodging-room with two single beds, a sort of lumber room and a small low unceiled room which I have papered with newspapers, and in which we have put a small bed without curtains.

Dorothy gardened passionately and idiosyncratically. Ferns and little flowers were transported from the woods and fields so as to smooth away any sense of division between countryside and house, and neighbours gave plants from their own stock. Her journal records a number of acquisitions: 'white and yellow lilies, periwinkle'; 'I planted London pride upon the wall'; 'I brought home lemon thyme and several other plants, and planted them by moonlight'; 'I rambled on the hill above the house gathered wild thyme and took up roots of wild columbine'. On one occasion she had a tremor of guilt:

> I found a strawberry blossom in a rock. The little slender flower had more courage than the green leaves, for *they* were but half expanded and half grown, but the blossom was spread

BELOW *Dorothy wrote to Jane Marshall of 'a small low unceiled room, which I have papered with newspapers and in which we have put a small bed without curtains'.*

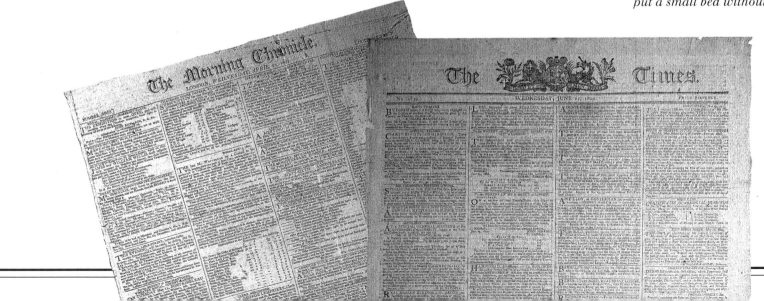

full out. I uprooted it rashly, and I felt as if I had been committing an outrage, so I planted it again. It will have but a stormy life of it, but let it live if it can.

The two young people (William was twenty-nine and Dorothy celebrated her twenty-eighth birthday on Christmas Day, just after their arrival at Dove Cottage) were buoyed up with a heady sense of freedom to act just as they chose. Sometimes they would walk by night, covering enormous distances, and then sleep all the next morning; sometimes they spent whole days lying in the orchard, reading aloud or reciting William's poems. They were very poor, often hungry, but entirely content with their lot and with each other.

Impressions of their daily life, interwoven with minute observations of nature and wonderfully fresh images, spring

RIGHT *Well at Skelgill by William Green, 1809.*
'All round this pool both flocks and herds might drink / On its firm margin, even as from a well / Or some stone-basin which the Herdsman's hand / Had shaped for their refreshment.': from a poem Wordsworth wrote to his future wife, Mary Hutchinson. Dorothy gathered ferns and mosses from just such spots to plant in her garden.

with startling clarity from the pages of Dorothy's journal and make hers the dominant narrative voice for the early Dove Cottage years. The journal's first entry, 14 May 1800, was written during an absence of William and their brother John, who was staying at Dove Cottage: 'I resolved to write a journal of the time till W. and J. return, and I set about keeping my resolve because I will not quarrel with myself, and because I shall give Wm pleasure by it when he comes home again.' A characteristically selfless motive. She noted the moon shining 'like herrings in the water'; of skeletal trees, she remarked, 'what a beautiful thing God has made winter to be by stripping the trees and letting us see their shapes and forms. What a freedom does it seem to give to the storms!' She described a raven as at once a real bird and a mysterious presence:

> After tea we rowed down to Loughrigg Fell, visited the white foxglove, gathered wild strawberries, and walked up to view Rydale . . . We heard a strange sound in the Bainriggs wood . . . it *seemed* in the wood, but it must have been above it, for presently we saw a raven very high above us—it called out and the dome of the sky seemed to echo the sound—it called again and again as it flew onwards, and the mountains gave back the sound, seeming as if from their centre a musical bell-like answering to the bird's hoarse voice. We heard both the call of the bird and the echo after we could see him no longer.

She recorded that a rainy morning showed 'our favourite Birch tree' in a new light:

> It was yielding to the gusty wind with all its tender twigs, the sun shone upon it and it glanced in the wind like a flying sunshiny shower. It was a tree in shape with stem and branches but it was like a spirit of water.

ABOVE *Strawberry plant. 'After tea we rowed down to Loughrigg Fell,' wrote Dorothy in July 1800, 'visited the white foxglove, gathered wild strawberries, and walked up to view Rydale.'*

She continued more prosaically that 'After tea Wm read Spenser now and then a little aloud to us. We were making his waistcoat.' Then she returned to her more visionary voice as she told of encountering William later in the evening in an agitated state, having been 'surprised and terrified by a sudden rushing of winds which seemed to bring earth sky and lake together, as if the whole were going to enclose him in'.

LEFT *Silhouette of Dorothy Wordsworth from Dove Cottage, probably made soon after her arrival there. In 'Home at Grasmere' William paid loving tribute to his sister: 'Wher'er my footsteps turned, / Her voice was like a hidden bird that sang, / The thought of her was like a flash of light / Or an unseen companionship, a breath / Of fragrance independent of the wind.' And Coleridge wrote that 'in her every motion her most innocent soul out-beams so brightly, that who saw her would say, "Guilt was a thing impossible with her."'*

LEFT *The Rock of Names, the Old Road, Thirlmere, by Henry Goodwin. Here William, Dorothy and John Wordsworth, Mary and Sara Hutchinson and Samuel Taylor Coleridge carved their initials in celebration of their mutual love. Two years later Coleridge deepened the initials with his penknife. 'I kissed them all,' declared Dorothy. 'We sat afterwards on the wall, seeing the sun go down on the reflections in the still water.' In 1880 the Manchester Water Authority blasted the rock during road making. Only fragments have survived.*

The journal tells of a whole spectrum of activities: Dorothy made straw mattresses and shoes; bottled rum; cooked; dug the garden; copied William's poems; and read aloud. Her health was often poor; her teeth fell out ('They will soon be gone. Let that pass, I shall be beloved—I want no more', she commented philosophically); long letters were written.

William and Dorothy's close companionship did not preclude other affectionate ties: the Wordsworths' hospitality was warm and unforced, their sense of family and of friendship intensely strong. During that first enchanted year their brother John was with them from January until September, walking, fishing, gardening and endearing himself to William and Dorothy by his quiet and modest nature; Mary Hutchinson paid a month's visit; and, to everyone's joy, Coleridge appeared in April, followed later by Mary's sister Sara. These especially precious intimates were received into a joyful communion of like-minded souls, a relationship sealed during the summer of 1800 with the carving of the initials of all six on a rock beside Thirlmere, which they called their 'Rock of Names': WW MH DW STC JW SH.

Meanwhile, Wordsworth worked steadily. He found writing a painful ordeal and dictated many of his poems to Dorothy. He preferred to compose out of doors and there are accounts of him pacing to and fro by the hour declaiming his verse. Sometimes he would work on little shared experiences, noted by Dorothy in her journal, which would lie dormant in his mind for a period of time—often as much as two years—before being transmuted into verse. One such episode was recorded by Dorothy in June 1800:

> On Tuesday, May 27th, a very tall woman, tall much beyond the measure of tall women, called at the door. She had on a very long brown cloak, and a very white cap without bonnet—her face was excessively brown, but it had plainly once been fair. She led a little bare-footed child about two years old by the hand and said her husband who was a tinker was gone before with the other children. I gave her a piece of bread. Afterwards on my road to Ambleside, beside the bridge at Rydale, I saw her husband sitting by the roadside, his two asses feeding beside him and the two young children at play upon the grass. The man did not beg. I passed on and about a quarter of a mile further I saw two boys before me, one about ten the other about eight years old at play chasing a butterfly. They were wild figures, not very ragged, but without shoes

LEFT *Silhouette of Sara Hutchinson in Wordsworth and Coleridge's silhouette book. Sara, Mary Hutchinson's sister and the beloved subject of Coleridge's 'Asra' poems, was small, with masses of auburn hair, and had an attractive vitality and quickness of perception. She later became a permanent member of the Wordsworth household, after her sister's marriage to Wordsworth.*

and stockings; the hat of the elder was wreathed round with yellow flowers, the younger whose hat was only a rimless crown, had stuck it round with laurel leaves. They continued at play till I drew very near and then they addressed me with the beggars' cant and the whining voice of sorrow. I said I served your mother this morning. (The boys were so like the woman who had called at the door that I could not be mistaken.) O! says the elder you could not serve my mother for she's dead and my father's on at the next town—he's a potter. I persisted in my assertion and that I would give them nothing. Says the elder Come, let's away, and away they flew like lightning.

William's poem 'Beggars' was composed two years after the encounter.

RIGHT *Travellers by John Harden. Many such itinerants, beggars, pedlars, tinkers, discharged soldiers and sailors, passed through Grasmere and were never turned away empty-handed by the Wordsworths, who listened sympathetically to their stories. Wordsworth spoke of one such character, the old leech gatherer, in 'Resolution and Independence': 'In my mind's eye I seemed to see him pace / About the weary moors continually, / Wandering about alone and silently.'*

The close relationship between the prose account and the subsequent poem is clear.

> *I left her, and pursued my way;*
> *And soon before me did espy*
> *A pair of little Boys at play,*
> *Chasing a crimson butterfly;*
> *The taller followed with his hat in hand,*
> *Wreathed round with yellow flowers the*
> *   gayest of the land.*
>
> *The other wore a rimless crown*
> *With leaves of laurel stuck about;*
> *And while both followed up and down,*
> *Each whooping with a merry shout,*
> *In their fraternal features I could trace*
> *Unquestionable lines of that wild Suppliant's face.*

Coleridge, entranced with his surroundings and companions, and unable to tear himself from Wordsworth's society, rented Greta Hall, a large house on the edge of Keswick, to which he moved his wife and child during the summer of 1800. The dozen or so miles of mountainous road separating the households proved no barrier to the friends, who strode between the two with exhilaration. The Coleridges stayed at Dove Cottage before the move and part of a letter written by Coleridge in July 1800 to his friend Humphry Davy, the young chemist and would-be poet, gives the flavour of that first Grasmere summer:

> We drank tea the night before I left Grasmere on the Island in that lovely lake, our kettle swung over the fire hanging from the branch of a Fir Tree, and I lay and saw the woods, and mountains, and lake all trembling, and as it were *idealized* thro' the subtle smoke which rose up from the clear red embers of the fir-apples which we had collected. Afterwards,

RIGHT *Keswick Lake looking towards Lodore Falls by Francis Towne, 1805. On arriving at Greta Hall Coleridge, enraptured with his surroundings, wrote to William Godwin: 'I question if there be a room in England which commands a view of Mountains and Lakes and Woods and Vales superior to that in which I am now sitting.' To Sara Hutchinson he spoke of the Lodore Falls as 'the Precipitation of the fallen angels from Heaven, Flight and Confusion and Distraction but all harmonized into one majestic Thing'.*

LEFT *Bonfire at night by W. H. Pyne. The figures silhouetted against the flames are reminiscent of Coleridge's description of the bonfire with the Wordsworths after their idyllic picnic together on the island in Grasmere Lake. Dorothy also recorded this 'great fire'.*

we made a glorious Bonfire on the Margin, by some alder bushes, whose twigs heaved and sobbed in the uprushing column of smoke—and the Image of the Bonfire, and of us that danced round it—ruddy laughing faces in the twilight—the Image of this in a Lake smooth as that sea, to whose waves the Son of God had said, PEACE! May God and all His Sons love you as I do—

S. T. Coleridge

Sara desires her kind remembrances—Hartley is a spirit that dances on an aspin leaf—the air, which yonder sallow-faced and yawning Tourist is breathing, is to my Babe a perpetual Nitrous Oxyde. Never was more joyous creature born.

Hartley Coleridge was by now four years old. Precocious, articulate, volatile, he was his father's darling and had inherited something of the latter's metaphysical turn of mind, as shown in an entry from Coleridge's notebooks:

March 17, 1801. Tuesday—Hartley looking out of my study window fixed his eyes steadily and for some time on the opposite prospect, and then said—Will yon Mountains *always* be?— I shewed him the whole magnificent Prospect in a Looking Glass, and held it up, so that the whole was like a Canopy or Ceiling over his head, and he struggled to express himself concerning the Difference between the Thing and the Image almost with convulsive Effort.—I never before saw such an Abstract of *Thinking* as a pure act and energy, of *Thinking* as distinguished from *Thoughts*.

Wordsworth, too, loved Hartley, addressing him as an 'exquisitely wild' being,

> *that dost float*
> *In such clear water, that thy boat*
> *May rather seem*
> *To brood on air than on an earthly stream;*
> *. . . I think of thee with many fears*
> *For what may be thy lot in future years.*

Hartley was never to lose his capacity for attracting affectionate concern, although Wordsworth's anxiety for him proved prophetic.

To his friend James Webbe Tobin, Coleridge wrote ecstatically about the prospect from his new home:

> Friday, July 25, 1800
>
> From the leads on the housetop of Greta Hall, Keswick, Cumberland, at the present time in the occupancy and usufruct-possession of S. T. Coleridge, Esq., Gentleman-poet and Philosopher in a mist.
>
> Yes, my dear Tobin, here I am, with Skiddaw behind my back; the Lake of Bassenthwaite, with its simple and majestic *case* of mountains, on my right hand; on my left, and stretching

ABOVE *Hartley Coleridge aged ten after a painting by David Wilkie. Hartley, Coleridge's eldest child and especial favourite, was brilliant, questioning and imaginative, showing from an early age an affinity with his father's metaphysical turn of mind. Coleridge wrote: 'Playfellows are burthensome to him—excepting me—because I can understand and sympathize with his wild Fancies.' Dorothy called him an 'original sprite'.*

far away into the fantastic mountains of Borrowdale, the Lake of Derwentwater; straight before me a whole camp of giants' tents,—or is it an ocean rushing in, in billows that, even in the serene sky, reach halfway to heaven? . . . Wordsworth remains at Grasmere till next summer (perhaps longer). His cottage is indeed in every respect so delightful a residence, the walks so dry after the longest rains, the heath and a silky kind of fern so luxurious a bedding on every hilltop, and the whole vicinity so tossed about on those little hills at the feet of the majestic mountains, that he moves in an eddy; he cannot get out of it . . Hartley returns his love to you; he talks often about you. I hear his voice at this moment distinctly; he is below in the garden, shouting to some foxgloves and fern, which he has transplanted, and telling them what he will do for them if they grow like good boys! This afternoon I sent him naked into a shallow of the river Greta; he trembled with the novelty, yet you cannot conceive his raptures.

God bless you!

I remain, with affectionate esteem,

Yours sincerely, S. T. Coleridge.

BELOW *Foxgloves, with their woodland habitats, were especially dear to Dorothy's heart. She could sit 'under the oak trees upon the mossy stones' and admire 'all things soft and green'.*

At about this time Coleridge began to suffer bouts of depression, from which he sought relief in laudanum and alcohol. Despite this ominous proclivity, he and Wordsworth collaborated on a new edition of *Lyrical Ballads* and on its famous Preface, Coleridge claiming later that he had provided Wordsworth with some of its most important phrases, including the celebrated definition of the genesis of poetry as 'emotion recollected in tranquillity'.

There are a number of references to the progress of their work in Dorothy's journal. She wrote:

All the morning I was busy copying poems. Gathered peas, and in the afternoon Coleridge came, very hot, he brought the second volume of the *Anthology*. The men went to bathe, and we afterwards sailed down to Loughrigg. Read poems on the water, and let the boat take its own course . . . At eleven o'clock Coleridge came when I was walking in the still clear moonshine in the garden. He came over Helvellyn . . . We sat and chatted till half past three, W. in his dressing gown. Coleridge read us a part of 'Christabel' . . . We walked in the wood by the lake. W. read 'Joanna' and 'The Fir Grove' to Coleridge . . . After dinner Coleridge discovered a rock-seat in the orchard. Cleared away the brambles. Coleridge obliged to go to bed after tea . . . I broiled Coleridge a mutton chop which he ate in bed.

ABOVE *Bassenthwaite Lake, a watercolour by James Bourne. The Wordsworths, in the course of their night-time rambles, would have seen the lake under this aspect. Wordsworth loved 'the varied solemnities of night', as he said in* Guide to the Lakes, *when 'the narrowness of the vales, and comparative smallness of the lakes, are especially adapted to bring surrounding objects home to the eye and to the heart.'*

Coleridge wrote in his notebooks after the bramble-clearing afternoon of 'the beards of thistle and dandelions flying above the lonely mountains like life'.

In August Coleridge reported back on his growing celebrity to Thomas Poole:

I was standing on the very top of Skiddaw, by a little Shed of Slate-stones on which I had scribbled with a bit of slate my name among the other names—a lean expressive-faced Man came up the Hill, stood beside me, a little while, then running over the names, exclaim[ed,] *Coleridge!* I lay my life, that is the *Poet Coleridge.*

At the beginning of the following month Dorothy attended a pauper's funeral:

Coleridge Wm and John went from home to go upon Helvellyn with Mr Simpson. They set out after breakfast. I accompanied them up near the blacksmith's. A fine coolish morning. I ironed till half past three—now very hot. I then went to a

ABOVE *Drawing, probably by Amos Green, inscribed 'Benjamin Tyson's cottage, Greenside Leadmines, Ullswater, 17 August 1848'. Ullswater was Wordsworth's 'most sublime' lake, the scene of a number of his boyhood exploits. The black lead from the local mines was used in the manufacture of pencils.*

funeral at John Dawson's. About ten men and four women. Bread cheese and ale. They talked sensibly and cheerfully about common things. The dead person 56 years of age buried by the parish. The coffin was neatly lettered and painted black and covered with a decent cloth. They set the corpse down at the door and while we stood within the threshold the men with their hats off sang with decent and solemn countenances a verse of a funeral psalm. The corpse was then borne down the hill and they sang till they had got past the town-end. I was affected to tears while we stood in the house, the coffin lying before me. There were no near kindred, no children. When we got out of the dark house the sun was shining and the prospect looked so divinely beautiful as I never saw it. It seemed more sacred than I had ever seen it, and yet more allied to human life. The green fields, neighbours of the churchyard, were as green as possible and with the brightness of the sunshine looked quite gay. I thought she was going to a quiet spot and I could not help weeping very much. When we came to the bridge they began to sing again and stopped during four lines before they entered the churchyard. The priest met us—he did not look as a man ought to do on such an occasion—I had seen him half-drunk the day before in a pot-house. Before we came with the corpse one of the company observed he wondered what sort of cue 'our parson would be in'. N.B. it was the day after the fair.

Later in the month John had to rejoin his ship. He was destined never to return to the Lakes. Dorothy spoke of her heart being 'right sad'. The departure of his brother, the 'silent poet' as he called him, was a sad deprivation for her and William. 'We were in view of the head of Ullswater,' Dorothy wrote, 'and stood till we could see him no longer, watching him as he *hurried* down the stony mountain.'

Coleridge now found himself unable to complete 'Christabel', his planned contribution to the new edition of

Lyrical Ballads. 'Every line,' he told his friend Tobin, 'has been produced by me with labor-pangs.' On 5 October Dorothy, referring to a second reading of the poem's first part, wrote, 'we had increasing pleasure.' However, the next day there was a laconic entry: 'Determined not to print "Christabel" with the *Lyrical Ballads.*' There were various reasons for this—the poem was unfinished, and it was also conspicuously different in genre from the rest of the collection.

On the surface, Coleridge accepted the decision philosophically, but he began to suffer from nightmares, probably opium-induced, and possibly stemming in part from his failure to compose, added to the tensions generated by his growing obsession with Sara Hutchinson. His notebook entry for 28 November reflected his sense of rejection:

> a most frightful Dream of a Woman whose features were blended with darkness catching hold of my right eye and attempting to pull it out—I caught hold of her arm fast—a horrid feel—Wordsworth cried out aloud to me hearing my scream—heard his cry and thought it cruel he did not come but did not wake till his cry was repeated a third time—the Woman's name Ebon Ebon Thalud.

He wrote pathetically to William Godwin:

> The Poet is dead in me—my imagination (or rather the Somewhat that had been imaginative) lies, like a Cold Snuff on the circular Rim of a Brass Candle-stick, without even a stink of Tallow to remind you that it was once cloathed and mitred with Flame. That is past by!—I was once a Volume of Gold Leaf, rising and riding on every breath of Fancy—but I have beaten myself back into weight and density, and now I sink in quicksilver, yea, remain squat and square on the earth amid the hurricane, that makes Oaks and Straws join in one Dance, fifty yards high in the Element.

LEFT *View of Newlands and part of Keswick Lake. Wordsworth commented: 'The general surface of the mountains is turf, rendered rich and green by the moisture of the climate. Sometimes the turf, as in the neighbourhood of Newlands, is little broken, the whole covering being soft and downy pasturage.'*

As a replacement for 'Christabel' Wordsworth wrote 'Michael', working against time and under such pressure that his health began to suffer. At the heart of the poem lay one of his central beliefs: the importance of harmony between man and nature, particularly as epitomized by the sheep-farmers, like Michael himself, who made up the core of the Grasmere neighbourhood and whose devotion to their flocks and way of life seemed to him a moral force for good. He and Dorothy, themselves living with the utmost frugality (they gratefully accepted gifts of cast-off clothing, or a barrel of flour), felt a sense of community with such neighbours.

In the poem the shepherd Michael's only son falls into disgrace and is exiled. Michael, sorrowing, seeks solace in the building of a sheep-fold:

RIGHT *Grasmere Church. Dorothy attended a village funeral on 3 September 1800. 'When we got out of the dark house the sun was shining . . . The green fields, neighbours of the churchyard, were as green as possible and with the brightness of the sunshine looked quite gay. I thought she was going to a quiet spot and I could not help weeping very much. When we came to the bridge they began to sing again and stopped during four lines before they entered the churchyard.'*

> *There is a comfort in the strength of love;*
> *'Twill make a thing endurable, which else*
> *Would overset the brain, or break the heart:*
> *I have conversed with more than one who well*
> *Remember the old Man, and what he was*
> *Years after he had heard this heavy news.*
> *His bodily frame had been from youth to age*
> *Of an unusual strength. Among the rocks*
> *He went, and still looked up to sun and cloud,*
> *And listened to the wind; and, as before,*
> *Performed all kinds of labour for his sheep,*
> *And for the land, his small inheritance.*
> *And to that hollow dell from time to time*
> *Did he repair, to build the Fold of which*
> *His flock had need.*

Wordsworth sent a copy of *Lyrical Ballads* to Charles James Fox, who had long been a hero of the poet for his humanitarian views. The accompanying letter set out the volume's purpose, especially in the case of 'The Brothers' and 'Michael':

LEFT *Manuscript of the opening lines of 'Michael', the composition of which caused Wordsworth so much distress. 'If from the public way you turn your steps / Up the tumultuous brook of Greenhead Ghyll, / You will suppose that with an upright path / Your feet must struggle; in such bold ascent / The pastoral mountains front you, face to face, / But, courage! for around that boisterous brook / The mountains have all opened out themselves, / And made a hidden valley of their own.'*

I have attempted to draw a picture of the domestic affections, as I know they exist amongst a class of men who are now almost confined to the north of England. They are small independent *proprietors* of land, here called statesmen, men of respectable education, who daily labour on their own little properties . . . You have felt that the most sacred of all property is the property of the poor. The two poems, which I have mentioned, were written with a view to show that men who do not wear fine clothes can feel deeply.

The early months of 1801 brought no alleviation for Coleridge, who resorted more and more to opium, including large quantities of the addictive Kendal Black Drop, an opium-based painkiller readily available in the neighbourhood, which he mixed liberally with brandy. He was anxious and depressed, harassed by debt, unhappy in his domestic life and comforted

ABOVE *Rocks on Loughrigg side.
Wordsworth recalled that while
Dorothy 'was sitting alone one
day, high up on this part of
Loughrigg Fell, she was so affected
by the voice of the cuckoo, heard
from the crags at some distance,
that she could not suppress a wish
to have a stone inscribed with her
name among the rocks from which
the sound proceeded'.*

only by Sara Hutchinson's sympathy. His nightmares continued, he suffered distressing physical symptoms, from boils to kidney troubles. The future seemed without hope. In April Dorothy wrote to Mary Hutchinson about his condition and the inadequacies of Mrs Coleridge as a nurse, although she pitied her as the poet's wife,

> for when one party is ill matched the other necessarily must be so too. She would have made a very good wife to many another man, but for Coleridge!! Her radical fault is want of sensibility, and what can such a woman be to Coleridge?

His little sons remained his chief solace during these troubled times. To Southey, always kind and sympathetic where children were concerned, he wrote of Hartley's promotion from smocks to boys' clothes:

> Hartley was breeched last Sunday—and looks far better than in his petticoats. He ran to and fro in a sort of dance to the Jingle of the Load of Money, that had been put in his breeches pockets; but he did [not] roll and tumble over and over in his old joyous way—No! it was an *eager* and solemn gladness, as if he felt it to be an awful aera in his Life.—O bless him! bless him! bless him! If my wife loved me, and I my wife, half as well as we both love our children, I should be the happiest man alive—but this is not—will not be!—

Escaping from domestic unease, Coleridge spent a clandestine summer holiday with the Hutchinson sisters at their brother's farmhouse, Gallow Hill. Here he was petted, coaxed and teased back to a state of comparative health by Mary and Sara in what seems on their side to have been an artlessly affectionate playfulness. Coleridge found the girls' innocent warmth piercingly delicious and in 'A Day-Dream' he looked back on their firelit kitchen as a sanctuary of bliss:

COOM GILL

My eyes make pictures, when they are shut:—
I see a fountain, large and fair,
A willow and a ruined hut,
And thee, and me and Mary there.
O Mary! make thy gentle lap our pillow!
Bend o'er us, like a bower, my beautiful green willow! . . .

O ever—ever, be thou blest!
For dearly, Asra, love I thee!
This brooding warmth across my breast,
This depth of tranquil bliss—ah me!
Fount, tree and shed are gone, I know not whither,
But in one quiet room we three are still together . . .

Thine eyelash on my cheek doth play—
'Tis Mary's hand upon my brow!
But let me check this tender lay
Which none may hear but she and thou!
Like the still hive at quiet midnight humming,
Murmur it to yourselves, ye two beloved women.

Later, Dorothy recorded Coleridge's departure for London:

C. had a sweet day for his ride. Every sight and every sound reminded me of him dear dear fellow—of his many walks to us by day and by night—of all dear things. I was melancholy and could not talk, but at last I eased my heart by weeping—nervous blubbering says William. It is not so.

By the end of the year she could write less distractedly:

The birches on the crags beautiful, red brown and glittering—the ashes glittering spears with their upright stems—the hips very beautiful, and so good!! and dear Coleridge—I ate twenty for thee when I was by myself.

LEFT Dorothy described 'our favourite Birch tree' seen through rain: 'It was yielding to the gusty wind with all its tender twigs, the sun shone upon it and it glanced in the wind like a flying sunshiny shower. It was a tree in shape with stem and branches but it was like a spirit of water.'

DOVE COTTAGE

THE GREAT CREATIVE YEAR

WILLIAM AND MARY had found increasing delight in each other's company during the autumn of 1801. Dorothy wrote of them as 'chearful, blossoming and happy', and her journal for 16 November recorded that 'Molly has been very witty with Mary all day. She says "Ye may say what ye will but there's nothing like a gay auld man for behaving weel to a young wife".' The old servant's cryptic utterance is perhaps explained by the fact that William looked old for his age: he and Mary were both thirty-one at the time. Their happiness was in cruel contrast to the situation of Coleridge, and the predominant impression at the end of 1801 was of Wordsworth's genius waxing as Coleridge's faltered and waned.

February 1802 brought bitterly cold weather and disturbing news of Coleridge. On 6 February Dorothy wrote dejectedly:

> William had slept badly. It snowed in the night, and was, on Saturday, as Molly expressed it, a Cauld Clash. William went to Rydale for letters, he came home with two very affecting letters from Coleridge—resolved to try another climate. I was stopped in my writing, and made ill by the letters. William a bad headache, he made up a bed on the floor, but could not sleep—I went to his bed and slept not—better when I rose.

Two days later William and Dorothy collected their letters:

> We broke the seal of Coleridge's letter, and I had light enough just to see that he was not ill. I put it in my pocket but at the

RIGHT *Rydal waterfall by Joseph Wright of Derby. Early in May 1802 William and Dorothy met Coleridge and together they rested near a waterfall. 'It is a glorious wild solitude under that lofty purple crag . . . A bird at the top of the crags was flying round and round and looked in thinness and transparency, shape and motion like a moth. We came down and rested on a moss covered rock, rising out of the bed of the river . . . Wm and C. repeated and read verses. I drank a little brandy and water and was in Heaven.'*

top of the White Moss I took it to my bosom, a safer place for it. The night was wild.

On a fine evening of that same cold month Dorothy passed a little group of travellers, who were to be immortalized in one of her vivid pictures:

About twenty yards above Glowworm Rock I met a carman, a Highlander I suppose, with four carts, the first three belonging to himself, the last evidently to a man and his family who had joined company with him and who I guessed to be potters. The carman was cheering his horses, and talking to a little lass about ten years of age who seemed to make him her companion. She ran to the wall and took up a large stone to support the wheel of one of his carts, and ran on before with it in her arms to be ready for him. She was a beautiful creature and there was something uncommonly impressive in the lightness and joyousness of her manner. Her business seemed to be all pleasure—pleasure in her own motions—and the man looked at her as if he too was pleased and spoke to her in the same tone in which he spoke to his horses. There was a wildness in her whole figure, not the wildness of a mountain lass but a *road* lass, a traveller from her birth, who had wanted neither food nor clothes. Her mother followed the last cart with a lovely child, perhaps about a year old, at her back and a good-looking girl about fifteen years old walked beside her . . . Her husband was helping the horse to drag the cart up by pushing it with his shoulder.

The spring of 1802 was one of the great creative periods of William's life: during these miraculous months some thirty poems were written. Dorothy's journal at this time shone with happiness, as spring burst upon Grasmere Vale and William, her 'Beloved', was at her side. The rapport between brother and sister seems to have been extraordinarily perfect, each

absorbing impressions from the other as if by some kind of osmosis. The journal conveys this rare sympathy in entry after entry, notably in the account of Dorothy's walk near Brothers Water on Good Friday. She and William set out together in early sunshine after heavy rain, and as they walked Dorothy registered everything she saw as if she were making notes for a painting. The details accumulated and the canvas began to fill:

> We saw a fisherman in the flat meadow on the other side of the water. He came towards us and threw his line over the two arched bridge. It is a bridge of a heavy construction, almost bending inwards in the middle, but it is grey and there is a look of ancientry in the architecture of it that pleased me.

Presently they came to another bridge, where they rested:

> We observed arches in the water occasioned by the large stones sending it down in two streams. A sheep came plunging through the river, stumbled up the bank and passed close to us, it had been frightened by an insignificant little dog on the other side, its fleece dropped a glittering shower under its belly.

At the foot of Brothers Water William sat on the bridge and Dorothy continued her walk alone, delighted with all she saw around her:

> The water under the boughs of the bare old trees, the simplicity of the mountains and the exquisite beauty of the path. There was one grey cottage. I repeated 'The Glowworm' as I walked along. I hung over the gate, and thought I could have stayed for ever.

When she regained the bridge she found William writing a poem 'descriptive of the sights and sounds we saw and heard':

LEFT *Sowing and harrowing, a watercolour by J. H. Harding. Among the sights Dorothy recorded near Brothers Water on a bright Good Friday morning were people at work 'ploughing, harrowing and sowing—lasses spreading dung, a dog's barking now and then.*

ABOVE *Oak in Rydal Park. On her Good Friday walk Dorothy noticed: 'The hawthorn a bright green with black stems under the oak. The moss of the oak glossy.' And Wordsworth wrote in his poem 'To M. H.' (Mary Hutchinson, later his wife): 'Our walk was far among the ancient trees; / There was no road, nor any woodman's path; . . . / The spot was made by Nature for herself; / The travellers knew it not, and 'twill remain / Unknown to them; but it is beautiful.'*

There was the gentle flowing of the stream, the glittering lively lake, green fields without a living creature to be seen on them, behind us, a flat pasture with forty-two cattle feeding to our left the road leading to the hamlet, no smoke there, the sun shone on the bare roofs. The people were at work ploughing, harrowing and sowing—lasses spreading dung, a dog's barking now and then, cocks crowing, birds twittering, the snow in patches at the top of the highest hills, yellow palms, purple and green twigs on the birches, ashes with their glittering spikes quite bare. The hawthorn a bright green with black stems under the oak. The moss of the oak glossy. We then went on, passed two sisters at work, *they first passed us*, one with two pitch forks in her hand. The other had a spade. We had some talk with them. They laughed aloud after we were gone perhaps half in wantonness, half boldness. William finished his poem, before we got to the foot of Kirkstone.

This catalogue of simple happenings, minutely observed (there were 42 cattle) and recorded in plain language, conjured up the scene in all its joyful liveliness of sound, sight and warmth. William's poem had a similar power. It began:

> The Cock is crowing,
> The stream is flowing,
> The small birds twitter,
> The lake doth glitter,
> The green field sleeps in the sun;
> The oldest and youngest
> Are at work with the strongest;
> The cattle are grazing,
> Their heads never raising;
> There are forty feeding like one!

Words did not always flow as easily as at Brothers Water, and Dorothy was often worried by William's exhaustion in struggling to compose. She watched him closely, protecting him in a manner partly maternal, partly directly physical, always intense. The journal for 17 March shows her presence soothing the poet's way through a difficult day:

> I went and sat with W. and walked backwards and forwards in the orchard till dinner time—he read me his poem. I broiled beefsteaks. After dinner we made a pillow of my shoulder, I read to him and my beloved slept—I afterwards got him the pillows and he was lying with his head on the table when Miss Simpson came in. She stayed tea.

LEFT *Man and woman writing at a table by John Harden, reminiscent of William and Dorothy working closely together—he composing, she transcribing, sometimes fluently and sometimes with painful difficulty.*

Later Dorothy walked Miss Simpson home, returning 'quietly along the side of Rydale lake with quiet thoughts', and then went in seach of William again.

> We walked backwards and forwards between home and Oliffs till I was tired. William kindled and began to write the poem. We carried cloaks into the orchard and sat a while there, I left him and he nearly finished the poem. I was tired to death and went to bed before him—he came down to me and read the poem to me in bed.

It was as though she gave her own vitality to facilitate the making of the poem: as 'William kindled', she could allow herself to become aware of her own fatigue. When he was comfortably installed in the orchard, the muse upon him, she could leave him, finding herself 'tired to death'. But even then William needed her sympathetic ear, seeking her out in bed to listen to the poem.

This rare picture of a poet in the very act of creation seems the more striking for the matter-of-fact tone of the recording voice. On another occasion brother and sister 'walked to Butterlip How and backwards and forwards there'. On their return they fell into a state of trance-like harmony: 'After we came in we sat in deep silence at the window—I on a chair and William with his hand on my shoulder. We were deep in silence and love, a blessed hour.'

Their relationship is shown to have been the pivotal force in both their lives, but for neither was it exclusively so. For William there was his growing love for Mary; for Dorothy an intense devotion to Coleridge and to her brother John. But William retained her adoration, and Dorothy remained the guardian of his vision, the being closest to his heart. When William was away, Dorothy's heart ached for his return; and when he was with Mary, perhaps talking about marriage, joy at receiving news from him was mixed with pain.

RIGHT *Cottage in Ambleside engraved by William Green. An example of Wordsworth's ideal for Lakeland cottages, which he felt should be 'the colour of the native rock, out of which they have been built . . . so that these humble dwellings remind the contemplative spectator of a production of Nature'.*

Walked to T. Wilkinson's and sent for letters. The woman brought me one from Wm and Mary. It was a sharp windy night. Thomas Wilkinson came with me to Barton, and questioned me like a catechizer all the way. Every question was like the snapping of a little thread about my heart I was so full of thoughts of my half-read letter and other things. I was glad when he left me. Then I had time to look at the moon while I was thinking over my own thoughts.

Sometimes Dorothy's excessive sensibility towards her brother trembled on the verge of the self-destructive. The journal entry of 4 March showed her struggling to overcome a tangle of emotions over William's departure on a short visit to his friend William Calvert at Windy Brow:

Before we had quite finished breakfast Calvert's man brought the horses for Wm. We had a deal to do to shave—pens to make—poems to put in order for writing, to settle the dress pack up etc . . . Since he has left me (at half past eleven) it is now two I have been putting the drawers into order, laid by his clothes which we had thrown here and there and everywhere, filed two months' newspapers and got my dinner two boiled eggs and two apple tarts. I have set Molly on to clear the garden a little, and I myself have helped. I transplanted some snowdrops—the bees are busy—Wm has a nice bright day . . . Now for my walk. I will be busy, I will look well and be well when he comes back to me. O the darling! Here is one of his bitten apples! I can hardly find in my heart to throw it into the fire. I must wash myself, then off—I walked round the two lakes crossed the stepping stones at Rydale foot. Sat down where we always sit. I was full of thoughts about my darling. Blessings on him.

By 18 March her equanimity seems to have been restored, though she still felt herself to be unwell. For the rest of her life she was to suffer from intermittent gastric attacks accompanied by severe headaches:

I felt myself weak, and William charged me not to go to Mrs Lloyd's. I seemed indeed, to myself unfit for it but when he was gone I thought I would get the visit over if I could—So I ate a beef-steak thinking it would strengthen me so it did, and I went off . . . I went through the fields, and sat half an hour afraid to pass a cow. The cow looked at me and I looked at the cow and whenever I stirred the cow gave over eating. I was not very much tired when I reached Lloyds. I walked in the garden . . . They came with me as far as Rydale. As we came along Ambleside vale in the twilight—it was a grave evening—there was something in the air that compelled me to serious thought. . . . There was a vivid sparkling streak of light at this

ABOVE *Pencil portrait of Coleridge by George Dance, 21 March 1804, just before the poet's departure for Malta in search of health and renewed spirits.*

RIGHT *Wythburn Water showing the foreground peaks thrown into sharp relief by the early evening light.*

ABOVE Pencil drawing of William Calvert, brother of Wordsworth's benefactor Raisley Calvert. Generous and unconventional, Calvert had been a fellow student of Wordsworth at Hawkshead Grammar School and was now an admirer of the poet and his neighbour at Windy Brow, near Keswick.

end of Rydale water but the rest was very dark and Loughrigg fell and Silver How were white and bright as if they were covered with hoar frost . . . I had many many exquisite feelings and when I saw this lowly building in the waters among the dark and lofty hills, with that bright soft light upon it, it made me more than half a poet.

How touchingly modest is this last phrase from one with such a poetic soul. But the tone of the journal that spring was predominantly happy, even ecstatic.

On 4 May the Wordsworths set off to meet Coleridge, who had for the moment shaken off his depression, so that the carefree atmosphere of the Alfoxden days seemed to have returned:

We came down and rested upon a moss covered rock, rising out of the bed of the river. There we lay ate our dinner and stayed there till about four o'clock or later. Wm and C. repeated and read verses. I drank a little brandy and water and was in Heaven . . . We parted from Coleridge at Sara's Crag after having looked at the letters which C. carved in the morning. I kissed them all. Wm deepened the T with C's penknife . . . C. looked well and parted from us cheerfully, hopping up upon the side stones.

That evening Dorothy recited verses to William 'while he was in bed—he was soothed and I left him. "This is the spot" over and over again.' The incantatory poem runs:

This is the spot:—how mildly does the sun
Shine in between these fading leaves! the air
In the habitual silence of this wood
Is more than silent: and this bed of heath,
Where shall we find so sweet a resting place?
Come!—let me see thee sink into a dream
Of quiet thoughts,—protracted till thine eye

LEFT *Aira Force, one of the most magnificent of the waterfalls in the Lakes. Coleridge described a torrent, 'the white down fall of which glimmered thro' the Trees, that hang before it like bushy Hair over a madman's Eyes'. Wordsworth, earlier intoxicated by such rushing waters, had written: 'The sounding cataract / Haunted me like a passion.'*

*Be calm as water, when the winds are gone
And no one can tell whither.—My sweet friend!
We two have had such happy hours together
That my heart melts in me to think of it.*

In Easedale, Dorothy sat watching the two men at a waterfall, 'Wm flinging stones into the river whose roaring was loud even where I was. When they returned William was repeating the poem "I have thoughts that are fed by the sun"':

*I have thoughts that are fed by the sun.
The things which I see
Are welcome to me,
Welcome every one;
I do not wish to lie
Dead, dead,*

*Dead without any company;
Here alone on my bed,*

LEFT *Storm coming on Ullswater from John Glover's sketchbook. Wordsworth made an expedition along the banks of Ullswater in stormy weather. 'The wind blew strong, and drove the clouds forward, on the side of the mountain above our heads;—two storm-stiffened black yew-trees fixed our notice, seen through, or under the edge of, the flying mists:—the sheep moved about more quietly, or cowered beneath their sheltering places . . . the lake, clouds and mists were all in motion to the sound of sweeping winds . . . the whole lake driving onward like a great river.'*

With thoughts that are fed by the Sun,
And hopes that are welcome every one,
Happy am I.

On their way home it began to rain heavily. 'We saw a family of little children sheltering themselves under a wall before the rain came on. They sat in a row making a canopy for each other of their clothes.'

John's Grove, in the following extract, was a favourite fir grove where John Wordsworth had often walked, treading out a pathway later retraced by his brother and sister:

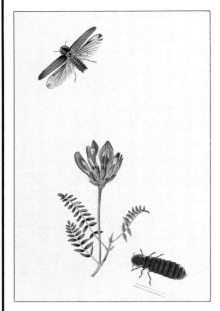

ABOVE *William wrote his glow-worm poem for Dorothy: 'Among all lovely things my Love had been; / Had noted well the stars, all flowers that grew / About her home; but she had never seen / A Glow-worm, never one, and this I knew.'*

The sun shone and all was pleasant. We sent off our parcel to Coleridge by the waggon . . . We then went to John's Grove, sat a while at first. Afterwards William lay, and I lay in the trench under the fence—he with his eyes shut and listening to the waterfalls and the birds. There was no one waterfall above another—it was a sound of waters in the air—the voice of the air. William heard me breathing and rustling now and then but we both lay still, and unseen by one another. He thought that it would be as sweet thus to lie so in the grave, to hear the *peaceful* sounds of the earth and just to know that our dear friends were near.

Coleridge had lain in a coffin-like declivity somewhere in the hills nearly a year earlier but, in contrast to the companionable proximity of the Wordsworths, his was a solitary experience:

'A Hollow place in the Rock like a Coffin—a Sycamore Bush at the head, enough to give a shadow for my Face, and just at the Foot one tall Foxglove—exactly my own Length—there I lay and slept —. It was quite soft.'

William's love for Dorothy is expressed in much of his work, notably in 'Tintern Abbey' and *The Prelude*. In April 1802 he sent Coleridge a particularly tender remembrance of her, based on an incident of seven years before:

ABOVE *Swallow-tail and brimstone on wild carrot and hawthorn by I. O. Westwood, 1841. 'Oh! pleasant, pleasant were the days' / The time, when in our childish plays, / My sister Emmeline and I / Together chased the butterfly! / A very hunter did I rush / Upon the prey;—with leaps and springs / I followed on from brake to bush; / But she, God love her! feared to brush / The dust from off its wings.' Emmeline was one of Wordsworth's pseudonyms for Dorothy.*

Among all lovely things my Love had been;
Had noted well the stars, all flowers that grew
About her home; but she had never seen
A Glow-worm, never one, and this I knew.

While riding near her home one stormy night
A single Glow-worm did I chance to espy;
I gave a fervent welcome to the sight,
And from my Horse I leapt; great joy had I.

Upon a leaf the Glow-worm did I lay,
To bear it with me through the stormy night:
And, as before, it shone without dismay;
Albeit putting forth a fainter light,

When to the Dwelling of my Love I came,
I went into the Orchard quietly;
And left the Glow-worm, blessing it by name,
Laid safely by itself, beneath a Tree.

The whole next day, I hoped, and hoped with fear;
At night the Glow-worm shone beneath the Tree:
I led my Lucy to the spot, 'Look here!'
Oh! Joy it was for her, and joy for me!

In his letter William described composing the poem as he rode home from a visit to Mary. Not surprisingly, he lost his way:

Soon after I missed my road in the midst of the storm, some people at a house where I called directed me how to regain the road through the fields, and alas! as you may guess I fared worse and worse . . . Unfortunately, not far from St. Helen's

ABOVE *Red admirals on thistles and nettles. William wrote: 'I've watched you now a full half hour, / Self-poised upon that yellow flower; / . . . How motionless! not frozen seas / More motionless! and then / What joy awaits you, when the breeze / Hath found you out among the trees, / And calls you forth again!'*

Auckland the Horse came down with me on his knees, but not so as to fall overhead himself or to throw me. Poor beast it was no fault of his!

Dorothy commented in her journal:

> Just when William came to a well or a trough which there is in Lord Darlington's park he began to write that poem of the glowworm . . . He did not feel the jogging of the horse while he was writing but when he had done he felt the effect of it and his fingers were cold with his gloves.

The second half of March was a time of extreme creativity for William and, in a journal account of the poet at work, the reader gains the impression of watching over his shoulder:

> William had slept badly—he got up at nine o'clock, but before he rose he had finished 'The Beggar Boys'—and while we were at breakfast that is (for I had breakfasted) he, with his basin of broth before him untouched and a little plate of bread and butter he wrote the poem to a butterfly! He ate not a morsel, nor put on his stockings but sat with his shirt neck unbuttoned, and his waistcoat open while he did it. The thought first came upon him as we were talking about the pleasure we both always feel at the sight of a butterfly. I told him that I used to chase them a little but that I was afraid of brushing the dust off their wings, and did not catch them—he told me how they used to kill all the white ones when he went to school because they were Frenchmen.

> *Oh! pleasant, pleasant were the days,*
> *The time, when in our childish plays,*
> *My sister Emmeline and I*
> *Together chased the butterfly!*
> *A very hunter did I rush*

Upon the prey;—with leaps and springs
I followed on from brake to bush;
But she, God love her! feared to brush
The dust from off its wings.

'Friday, William wrote to Annette then worked at the Cuckow,'
Dorothy wrote in her journal. 'I was ill and in bad spirits . . .
While I was getting into bed he wrote "The Rainbow"':

My heart leaps up when I behold
  A rainbow in the sky:
So was it when my life began;
So is it now I am a man;
So be it when I shall grow old,
  Or let me die!
The Child is father of the Man;
And I could wish my days to be
Bound each to each by natural piety.

LEFT *Wordsworth wrote: 'There is also an imaginative influence in the voice of the cuckoo, when that voice has taken possession of a deep mountain valley, very different from anything which can be excited by the same sound in a flat country.'*

The next day, 27 March, brought what is perhaps the most
astonishing entry in the journal: 'Saturday. A divine morning.
At breakfast Wm wrote part of an ode. Mr Olliff sent the dung
and Wm went to work in the garden. We sat all day in the
orchard.' Thus casually, and in the same breath as the load of
dung, Dorothy announced the inception of the first four stanzas
of the great 'Ode: Intimations of Immortality from Recollections
of Early Childhood'. The completed poem began:

There was a time when meadow, grove, and stream,
The earth, and every common sight,
    To me did seem
  Apparelled in celestial light,
The glory and the freshness of a dream.
It is not now as it hath been of yore;—
    Turn wheresoe'er I may,

By night or day,
The things which I have seen I now can see no more.

The Rainbow comes and goes,
And lovely is the Rose,
The Moon doth with delight
Look round her when the heavens are bare,
Waters on a starry night
Are beautiful and fair;
The sunshine is a glorious birth;
But yet I know, where'er I go,
That there hath past away a glory from the earth.

BELOW *Spring flowers by Mary Elizabeth Duffield. The first entry in Dorothy's journal, for 14 May 1800, tells of her intense joy at the wood rich in flowers: 'a beautiful yellow, palish yellow, flower that looked thick, round, and double, and smelt very sweet—I supposed it was a ranunculus. Crowfoot, the grassy-leaved rabbit-toothed white flower, strawberries, geranium, scentless violets, anemones two kinds, orchises, primroses.'*

Through these pages of the journal may be traced something of the movement of William's mind during the previous few days as he looked back on childhood hours chasing butterflies, first with Dorothy, later with schoolfriends; then, in 'The Rainbow', he declared his faith in the image of the rainbow as an arch linking childhood to manhood, so that a little of the innocent eye, the 'visionary gleam' of the child, would survive to illuminate the more complex vision of experience.

The only dark shadow on this idyllic time was cast by Coleridge's worsening state. His reading aloud of 'Letter to Sara Hutchinson', that anguished outpouring on the theme of tortured love, distressed the Wordsworths. They felt his sense of isolation and pain at belonging no more to that charmed circle of friends whose initials were carved on the Rock of Names:

To see thee, hear thee, feel thee—then to part
Oh! it weighs down the Heart!
To visit those, I love, as I love thee,
Mary, and William, and dear Dorothy,
It is but a temptation to repine—
The transientness is Poison in the Wine,
Eats out the pith of Joy, makes all Joy hollow,

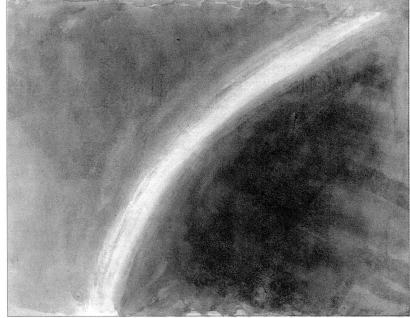

RIGHT *Sky study with rainbow, a watercolour by John Constable, 1827. 'My heart leaps up when I behold / A rainbow in the sky: / So was it when my life began; / So is it now I am a man; / So be it when I shall grow old, / Or let me die!'*

All Pleasure a dim Dream of Pain to follow!
My own peculiar Lot, my house-hold Life
It is, and will remain, Indifference or Strife—
While ye *are* well *and* happy, *'twould but wrong you*
If I should fondly yearn to be among you—
Wherefore, O wherefore! should I wish to be
A wither'd branch upon a blossoming Tree?

Dorothy was shattered by the poem:

Coleridge came to us and repeated the verses he wrote to Sara. I was affected with them and was on the whole, not being well, in miserable spirits. The sunshine—the green fields and the fair sky made me sadder.

67

RIGHT *Itinerant by John Harden. The Wordsworths encountered many such travellers on their walks. On one occasion, as they went up White Moss, Dorothy wrote: 'we met an old man who I saw was a beggar by his two bags hanging from his shoulder . . . I gave him a halfpenny. He was 75 years of age, had a freshish colour in his cheeks . . . He walked with a slender stick decently stout, but his legs bowed outwards.'*

During the spring William visited Mary, telling Dorothy on his return that he had found her looking thin and ill. This elicited loving reassurances from Dorothy:

My dear, dear Mary! I am deeply concerned to hear that you are so thin . . . Take no more exercise than would be proper for the regaining of your strength supposing that you were nearly as *weak* as you are *thin*—above all, my dearest Mary, seek quiet or rather amusing thoughts. Study the flowers, the birds and all the common things that are about you. O Mary, my dear Sister! be quiet and happy. Take care of yourself— keep yourself employed without fatigue, and do not make loving us your business, but let your love of us make up the spirit of all the business you have . . . Dear Mary, we are glad to be at home. No fireside is like this. Be chearful in the thought of coming to it.

William added, 'Heaven bless you, dearest Mary!'

'Resolution and Independence', known to the Dove Cottage circle as 'The Leech Gatherer', was completed in the early summer. William based the poem on an incident recorded in the journal of October 1800, when he and Dorothy had met 'an old man almost double':

he had on a coat thrown over his shoulders above his waistcoat and coat. Under this he carried a bundle and had an apron on and a night cap. His face was interesting. He had dark eyes and a long nose . . . His trade was to gather leeches, but now leeches are scarce and he had not strength for it. He lived by begging and was making his way to Carlisle where he should buy a few godly books to sell. He said leeches were very scarce partly owing to this dry season, but many years they have been scarce—he supposed it owing to their being much sought after, that they did not breed fast, and were of slow growth.

He told, that to these waters he had come
To gather leeches, being old and poor:
Employment hazardous and wearisome!
And he had many hardships to endure:
From pond to pond he roamed, from moor to moor;
Housing, with God's good help, by choice or chance;
And in this way he gained an honest maintenance.

William sent a draft of the poem to the Hutchinson sisters and Sara replied with a list of criticisms that brought an aggrieved response from William and a rebuke from Dorothy:

Dear Sara
When you happen to be displeased with what you suppose to be the tendency or moral of any poem which William writes, ask yourself whether you have hit upon the real tendency and true moral, and above all never think that he writes for no reason but merely because a thing happened—and when you feel any poem of his to be tedious, ask yourself in what spirit it was written—whether merely to tell the tale and be through with it, or to illustrate a particular character or truth.

Sara's criticisms were nevertheless acted upon in the final version.

Midsummer brought a miniature tragedy, recounted by Dorothy in her journal:

Friday June 25th. Wm had not fallen asleep till after three o'clock but he slept tolerably. Miss Simpson came to colour the rooms. I began with white-washing the ceiling. I worked with them (William was very busy) till dinner time but after dinner I went to bed and fell asleep. When I rose I went just before tea into the garden. I looked up at my swallow's nest and it was gone. It had fallen down. Poor little creatures they could not themselves be more distressed than I was. I went upstairs to look at the ruins. They lay in a large heap upon the

ABOVE *Interior with two women by John Harden, Brathay, 1804. Harden, of Brathay Hall, not far from the Wordsworths at Grasmere, was an amateur artist who depicted the everyday scenes around him, both domestic interiors such as this, and the outdoor life and landscapes of the Lakes.*

window ledge; these swallows had been ten days employed in building this nest, and it seemed to be almost finished. I had watched them early in the morning, in the day many and many a time and in the evenings when it was almost dark I had seen them sitting together side by side in their unfinished nest both morning and night. When they first came about the window they used to hang against the panes, with their white bellies and their forked tails looking like fish, but then they fluttered and sang their own little twittering song. As soon as the nest was broad enough, a sort of ledge for them they sat both mornings and evenings, but they did not pass the night there. I watched them one morning, when William was at Eusemere, for more than an hour. Every now and then there was a feeling motion in their wings, a sort of tremulousness and they sang a low song to one another.

BELOW *Dorothy wrote in her journal on 8 July 1802: 'I went to bed but did not sleep. The Swallows stole in and out of their nest, and sat there* whiles *quite still, whiles* they sung low for two minutes or more at a time just like a muffled Robin.'

During May and June William had written 'Farewell, thou little nook of mountain-ground', the poem Dorothy called 'Going for Mary'. It was at once a grateful farewell to a time and place of shared happiness and a gesture of welcome to his future wife:

RIGHT *View of London from Lambeth after Joseph Farington. This is the scene that inspired Wordsworth to write the sonnet that begins 'Earth has not anything to show more fair' as, having crossed Westminster Bridge early on a beautiful summer's morning, he travelled south on top of the Dover coach.*

> *We go for One to whom ye will be dear;*
> *And she will prize this Bower, this Indian shed,*
> *Our own contrivance, Building without peer!*
> *— A gentle Maid, whose heart is lowly bred,*
> *Whose pleasures are in wild fields gathered,*
> *With joyousness, and with a thoughtful cheer,*
> *Will come to you; to you herself will wed;*
> *And love the blessed life that we lead here.*

In the summer of 1802 arrangements for their marriage were under way; but the matter of William's early liaison with Annette Vallon remained unresolved. Letters had arrived from her during the spring, and the signing of the fragile Peace of Amiens at last made travel in France a possibility, leading

William to decide that he must see her again and meet his daughter Caroline. Whether his reason was to close an episode or to satisfy an impulse of romantic nostalgia cannot be known; but on 9 June brother and sister set off on the journey to France. They left London for Dover at the end of July. Dorothy's journal described their departure: 'We mounted the Dover Coach at Charing Cross. The City, St Paul's, with the river and a multitude of little boats, made a most beautiful sight as we crossed Westminster Bridge.' William's sonnet on the occasion was composed on top of the coach:

Earth has not anything to show more fair:
Dull would he be of soul who could pass by
A sight so touching in its majesty:
This City now doth, like a garment, wear
The beauty of the morning; silent, bare,
Ships, towers, domes, theatres, and temples lie
Open unto the fields, and to the sky;
All bright and glittering in the smokeless air.
Never did sun more beautifully steep
In his first splendour valley, rock, or hill;
Ne'er saw I, never felt, a calm so deep!
The river glideth at his own sweet will:
Dear God! The very houses seem asleep;
And all that mighty heart is lying still!

ABOVE *Shakespeare's Cliff, Dover.
On their return from France, and
their visit to Annette Vallon,
William and Dorothy 'sat upon
Dover cliffs and looked upon
France with many a melancholy
and tender thought. We could see
its shores almost as plain as if it
were but an English lake.' William
was to see Annette and his
daughter Caroline only twice more
in his life.*

Dorothy's journal for the month spent in Calais is tantalizingly uninformative. She briefly recorded their arrival, the dirty lodgings, the finding of Annette and Caroline; but of the emotions, painful or joyful, of the reunion she wrote nothing. She spoke of walks, bathing and one especially lovely evening recalled in her brother's sonnet 'It is a beauteous evening, calm and free', with its tender note of affection for his nine-year-old daughter:

Dear Child! dear Girl! that walkest with me here,
If thou appear untouched by solemn thought,
Thy nature is not therefore less divine:
Thou liest in Abraham's bosom all the year;
And worshipp'st at the Temple's inner shrine,
God being with thee when we know it not.

Annette was a brave woman, who had been a member of the resistance in the late wars and had given refuge to escaping Chouans, members of the Catholic and Royalist party. Whatever transpired at Calais, and whether William behaved with a culpable coldness, or whether a mutual decision was

RIGHT *Bartholomew Fair from R. Ackermann's* Microcosm of London, *1808. The Fair was described by Wordsworth in* The Prelude: *'All moveables of wonder, from all parts, / Are here—Albinos, painted Indians, Dwarfs, / The Horse of knowledge, and the learned Pig, / The Wax-work, Clock-work, all the marvellous craft / Of modern Merlins, Wild Beasts, Puppet-shows, / All jumbled up together, to compose / A Parliament of Monsters. Tents and Booths / Meanwhile, as if the whole were one vast mill, / Are vomiting, receiving on all sides, / Men, Women, three-years' Children, Babes in arms.'*

made to leave the past behind, remains a matter for conjecture. Annette and William met only twice more in their lives, but over the years a friendly relationship seems to have been maintained with mother and daughter, nurtured by Dorothy and the selfless Mary.

The Wordsworths returned to England at the end of August. Together they sat on Dover cliffs and looked upon France 'with many a melancholy and tender thought!' William's mind was determined on marriage with Mary, but these summer weeks must at the least have aroused disturbing memories of the promises made to Annette.

Before leaving the south William and Dorothy spent some time in London, lodging near Charles and Mary Lamb, who gave them a kind welcome. One evening Charles took them to Bartholomew Fair by Smithfield, a tumultuous experience described in *The Prelude*:

What a shock
For eyes and ears! what anarchy and din,
Barbarian and infernal,—a phantasma,
Monstrous in colour, motion, shape, sight, sound!

Lamb had refused the Wordsworths' invitation to Dove Cottage the previous year with a beguiling piece of special pleading:

> With you and your Sister I could gang any where. But I am afraid whether I shall ever be able to afford so desperate a Journey. Separate from the pleasure of your company, I don't much care if I never see a mountain in my life. I have passed all my days in London, until I have formed as many and intense local attachments, as any of you mountaineers can have done with dead nature. The Lighted shops of the Strand and Fleet Street, the innumerable trades, tradesmen and customers, coaches, waggons, playhouses, all the bustle and wickedness round about Covent Garden, the very women of the Town, the Watchmen, drunken scenes, rattles,—life awake, if you awake, at all hours of the night . . . the very dirt and mud, the Sun shining upon houses and pavements, the print shops, the old book stalls, parsons cheap'ning books, coffee houses, steams of soups from kitchens, the pantomimes, London itself a pantomime and a masquerade,—all these things work themselves into my mind and feed me, without a power of satiating me. The wonder of these sights impells me into night-walks about her crowded streets, and I often shed tears in the motley Strand from fulness of joy at so much Life.—All these emotions must be strange to you. So are your rural emotions to me.

But during the Wordsworths' visit to France the Lambs did venture north, arriving unannounced at Greta Hall, where Coleridge welcomed them and showed them the sights. Lamb reported their exploits to his friend Thomas Manning:

LEFT *Watenlath with the Falls of Lodore, a watercolour by Thomas Girtin. Even Lamb, the passionate Londoner, admired the beauty of these falls when he eventually came to the Lakes, and Southey wrote a poem about them. Coleridge wrote of 'great Masses of Water, one after the other, that in twilight one might have feelingly compared them to a vast crowd of huge whie Bears, rushing, one over the other, against the wind—their long whie hair shattering abroad in the wind.'*

RIGHT *Engraving of Charles Lamb, inscribed in his hand 'Yours ratherish unwell Chs Lamb'. Lamb drew back from the idea of visiting the Lakes. 'I have passed all my days in London, until I have formed as many and intense local attachments, as any of you mountaineers can have done with dead nature,' he protested to the Wordsworths.*

We have clambered up to the top of Skiddaw, and I have waded up the bed of Lodore. In fine, I have satisfied myself, that there is such a thing as that which tourists call *romantic*, which I very much suspected before: they make such a spluttering about it, and toss their splendid epithets around them, till they give as dim a light, as four o'clock next morning the lamps do after an illumination . . . It was a day that will stand out, like a mountain, I am sure, in my life.

A few days after Lamb's departure Coleridge sent an account of the Lodore falls to William Sotheby, the poet and translator. He had already described them to Sara Hutchinson as 'the Precipitation of the fallen Angels from Heaven, Flight and Confusion, and Distraction, but all harmonized into one majestic Thing by the genius of Milton.' Now to nature's brilliance he added that of his children dancing in the wind:

My Dear Sir,
The river is full, and Lodore is full, and silver fillets come out of clouds and glitter in every ravine of all the mountains; and the hail lies like snow, upon their tops, and the impetuous gusts from Borrowdale snatch the water up high, and continually at the bottom of the lake it is not distinguishable from snow slanting before the wind—and under this seeming snowdrift the sunshine *gleams*, and over all the nether half of the Lake it is *bright* and *dazzles*, a cauldron of melted silver boiling! It is in very truth a sunny, misty, cloudy, dazzling, howling, omniform day, and I have been looking at as pretty a sight as a father's eyes could well see—Hartley and little Derwent running in the green where the gusts blow most madly, both with their hair floating and tossing, a miniature of the agitated trees, below which they were playing, inebriate both with the pleasure—Hartley whirling round for joy, Derwent eddying, half-willingly, half by the force of the gust,—driven backward, struggling forward, and shouting his little hymn of joy.

LEFT *Greta Hall. Coleridge brought his family to this large and elegant house in 1800. The panorama of lakes and mountains seen from its elevated position gave the poet exquisite pleasure. His enthusiasm later brought the Southeys north to share the house.*

The happy children seemed to embody Coleridge's earlier dream for Hartley, as he had described it in 'Frost at Midnight', when, sitting by the dying fire late one night, with his baby son asleep in a cradle beside him, he had vowed that the child should have the privilege of growing up under the blessed tutelage of nature:

> But thou, *my babe! shalt wander like a breeze*
> *By lakes and sandy shores, beneath the crags*
> *Of ancient mountain, and beneath the clouds*
> *Which image in their bulk both lakes and shores*
> *And mountain crags*

so that he would come to live in tune with the spirit of God inherent in all things:

> *Therefore all seasons shall be sweet to thee,*
> *Whether the summer clothe the general earth*
> *With greenness, or the redbreast sit and sing*
> *Betwixt the tufts of snow on the bare branch*
> *Of mossy apple-tree, while the nigh thatch*
> *Smokes in the sun-thaw; whether the eave-drops fall*
> *Heard only in the trances of the blast,*
> *Or if the secret ministry of frost*
> *Shall hang them up in silent icicles,*
> *Quietly shining to the quiet Moon.*

The time had now come for William to set off for Yorkshire to meet his bride. He and Dorothy reached Gallow Hill, near Scarborough, where Mary lived with her farmer brother Tom, at the end of September. There they remained until after the wedding, Dorothy ill for the greater part of the visit, wrought to a nervous pitch by the emotional demands of the summer and of the impending marriage. She wrote bravely to her friend Jane Marshall:

LEFT *Manuscript page from Dorothy's journal, part of the entry for William's wedding day, 4 October 1802. 'At a little after eight o'clock I saw them go down the avenue towards the church. William had parted from me upstairs. I gave him the wedding ring—with how deep a blessing!' Emphatic scorings-out punctuate the passage.*

RIGHT *Skiddaw over Derwentwater. Lamb wrote to his friend Thomas Manning: 'We have clambered up to the top of Skiddaw, and I have waded up the bed of Lodore. In fine, I have satisfied myself, that there is such a thing as that which tourists call romantic . . . It was a day that will stand out, like a mountain, I am sure, in my life.'*

My dear Friend,

. . . We leave Gallow Hill on Monday morning, immediately after my Brother William's marriage, we expect to reach Grasmere on Wednesday Evening. William, Mary and I go together in a post chaise . . . I have long loved Mary Hutchinson as a Sister, and she is equally attached to me this being so, you will guess that I look forward with perfect happiness to this Connection between us, but, happy as I am, I half dread that concentration of all tender feelings, past, present, and future which will come upon me on the wedding morning. There never lived on earth a better woman than Mary H. and I have not a doubt but that she is in every respect formed to make an excellent wife to my Brother, and I seem to myself to have scarcely any thing left to wish for but that the wedding was over, and we had reached our home once again. We have, indeed, been a long time absent . . .

God bless you my dear Jane! Your affectionate and faithful friend,

D. Wordsworth.

Dorothy's account of the wedding day makes heart-breaking reading; with the return of William and Mary from Brompton Church as man and wife, she was describing what seemed to her the end of a halcyon age:

On Monday 4th October 1802, my brother William was married to Mary Hutchinson. I slept a good deal of the night and rose fresh and well in the morning. At a little after eight o'clock I saw them go down the avenue towards the church. William had parted from me upstairs. I gave him the wedding ring—with how deep a blessing! I took it from my forefinger where I had worn it the whole of the night before—he slipped it again onto my finger and blessed me fervently. When they were absent my dear little Sara prepared the breakfast. I kept myself as quiet as I could, but when I saw the two men

ABOVE *Silhouette of Mrs Wordsworth. Wordsworth wrote of his wife Mary: 'A perfect Woman, nobly planned / To warn, to comfort, and command; / And yet a spirit still, and bright, / With something of angelic light.' A few years later Coleridge could write: 'A blessed marriage for him and for her it has been.'*

RIGHT *Grasmere engraved after Joseph Farington. The vale to which William brought his bride in the autumn of 1802. Coleridge described it as 'tossed about on those little hills at the feet of the majestic mountains'. And William felt that '. . . a willing mind / Might almost think, at this affecting hour, / That paradise, the lost abode of man, / Was raised again.'*

running up the walk, coming to tell us it was over, I could stand it no longer and threw myself on the bed where I lay in stillness, neither hearing or seeing any thing, till Sara came upstairs to me and said 'They are coming'. This forced me from the bed where I lay and I moved I knew not how straight forward, faster than my strength could carry me till I met my beloved William and fell upon his bosom. He and John Hutchinson led me to the house and there I stayed to welcome my dear Mary. As soon as we had breakfasted we departed. It rained when we set off. Poor Mary was much agitated when she parted from her brothers and sisters and her home.

DOVE COTTAGE

*L*OVE AND *F*RIENDSHIP

N HER ARRIVAL as a bride at Dove Cottage Mary was at once taken into the garden to see its beauties by candle-light, thus fulfilling William's promise, written before setting out with Dorothy to fetch his bride:

RIGHT *Staveley, Westmorland, a watercolour by John Harden. Dorothy had an affection for Staveley, as the first mountain village she and William came to 'when we first began our pilgrimage together. Here we drank a basin of milk at a public house, and here I washed my feet in the brook and put on a pair of silk stockings by William's advice.'*

O happy Garden! whose seclusion deep
Hath been so friendly to industrious hours;
And to soft slumbers, that did gently steep
Our spirits, carrying with them dreams of flowers,
And wild notes warbled among leafy bowers;
Two burning months let summer over-leap.
And, coming back with Her who will be ours,
Into thy bosom we again shall creep.

Mary herself brought a comparably soothing influence to bear on the little ménage, and William and Dorothy derived benefit from her gentle calm. Perhaps because she now had a sympathetic confidante at hand, Dorothy allowed her journal to lapse. The final entry, of 16 January 1803, is typical of her delicate sensitivity to the feelings of others:

Intensely cold. Wm had a fancy for some gingerbread I put on Molly's Cloak and my spencer, and we walked towards Matthew Newton's. I went into the house. The blind man and his wife and sister were sitting by the fire, all dressed very clean in their Sunday's clothes, the sister reading. They took their little stock of gingerbread out of the cupboard and I bought six pennyworth. They were so grateful when I paid them for it that I could not find it in my heart to tell them we were going to make gingerbread ourselves.

It must have been hard for Dorothy to adjust to the new era at Dove Cottage, but there is nothing to suggest that the love she and Mary felt for one another was ever ruffled throughout a long life spent together. Mary's tact no doubt eased the transition and protected her sister-in-law from what might have become a painful sense of exclusion.

Towards the end of the bridal journey Dorothy had begun to dwell on memories of that first magical approach to Grasmere, alone with her brother. But there was joy in reaching Dove Cottage at last:

> I am always glad to see Staveley it is a place I dearly love to think of—the first mountain village that I came to with Wm when we first began our pilgrimage together. Here we drank a basin of milk at a public house, and here I washed my feet in the brook and put on a pair of silk stockings by Wm's advice.

Now, on their second arrival, 'Molly was overjoyed to see us, for my part I cannot describe what I felt, and our dear Mary's feelings would I dare say not be easy to speak of.' Two days later the women had already established a routine: 'On Friday 8th we baked bread, and Mary and I walked, . . . the first walk that I had taken with my sister.'

William, too, settled to work, composing a series of sonnets on public issues. And, in gentler mood, he also wrote a poem for his wife, 'She Was a Phantom of Delight', ending:

> A perfect Woman, nobly planned,
> To warn, to comfort, and command;
> And yet a Spirit still, and bright
> With something of angelic light.

In June 1803 Mary gave birth to her first son, Johnny. Dorothy waxed ecstatic over the baby, as she would later over all the young Wordsworths—'our children', as she possessively called

BELOW *Lady reading in a tree, a drawing by John Harden. Dorothy Wordsworth loved to read out of doors. Shakespeare and Chaucer were favourites, but she would read and re-read her brother's poems.*

them. She wrote to her close friend, Catherine Clarkson, wife of the anti-slavery campaigner:

> My dear Friend
> Mary and I have never ceased to regret that you did not see our own darling child before your departure from this country. It would have been very sweet to us to think that you had carried away an image of what we so dearly love . . . He has blue eyes, a fair complexion, (which is already very much sunburnt,) a body as fat as a little pig, arms that are thickening and dimpling and bracelets at his wrists, a very prominent nose, which *will be* like his Father's, and a head shaped upon the very same model. I send you a lock of his hair sewed to this letter. To-day we have all been at Church. Mary was *churched* and the Babe christened—Coleridge my Brother Richard, and I were Godfathers and Godmother, old Mr Sympson answered for my Brother Richard, and had a hearty enjoyment of the christening cake, tea and coffee, this afternoon. The Child sleeps all night, and is a very good sleeper in the day. I wish you could see him in his Basket which is neither more nor less than a meat Basket which costs half a crown. In this basket he has (Not like Moses in his cradle of rushes, but in a boat, mind that. W. W.) floated over Grasmere water asleep and made one of a dinner party at the Island, and we often carry it to the orchard-seat where he drops asleep beside us . . . God bless you my ever dear Friend . . .
> Yours ever and ever Dorothy Wordsworth.

LEFT *Picnic on Windermere by John Harden. A picnic such as that attended by the month-old John Wordsworth, William's first son. Dorothy wrote of his cradle being 'a meat Basket which costs half a crown. In this basket he has . . . floated over Grasmere water asleep and made one of a dinner party at the Island.' William protested in the margin of the letter: 'Not like Moses in his cradle of rushes, but in a boat, mind that. W.W.'*

Dorothy was also able to give Mrs Clarkson the good news that the late Lord Lonsdale's debt to the Wordsworths was at last to be repaid by his cousin and heir: 'We are to receive eight thousand five hundred pounds.' This had to be divided between all five of them, but nevertheless it did something to alleviate their precarious financial position. William wrote to his brother Richard, who had managed all the legal correspondence, to thank him. He added: 'We are going to make a tour of 6 weeks in Scotland, Dorothy I and Coleridge. Do not imagine we are going to launch out in expence, we expect it will do our healths good, and shall travel with one Horse only.'

The Scottish tour duly took place, with Mary and the baby left behind. It failed to re-create the excitement and stimulation of earlier expeditions; both men were unwell and moody, and they agreed to separate. But the journey generated one of the most beautiful of William's lyrics, the exquisite 'Solitary Reaper'. Dorothy mentioned in her account of the tour that 'It was harvest-time, and the fields were quietly . . . enlivened by small companies of reapers. It is not uncommon in the more lonely parts of the Highlands to see a *single* person so employed.' A passage in Wilkinson's *Tours to the British Mountains* was another source of inspiration for William, who did not complete the poem for more than two years after the tour: 'Passed by a Female who was reaping alone: she sung in Erse as she bended over her sickle; the sweetest human Voice I ever heard: her strains were tenderly melancholy and felt delicious, long after they were heard no more.' Echoes from both accounts were combined in the finished poem:

> *Behold her, single in the field,*
> *Yon solitary Highland Lass!*
> *Reaping and singing by herself;*
> *Stop here, or gently pass!*
> *Alone she cuts and binds the grain,*
> *And sings a melancholy strain;*
> *O Listen! for the Vale profound*
> *Is overflowing with the sound . . .*
>
> *Will no one tell me what she sings?—*
> *Perhaps the plaintive numbers flow*
> *For old, unhappy, far-off things,*
> *And battles long ago:*

ABOVE *Woman reaper, binding stems, a drawing by James Ward. Wordsworth had been inspired to write his 'Solitary Reaper' at the sight of such a figure on his Scottish tour: 'Alone she cuts and binds the grain, / And sings a melancholy strain; / O Listen! for the Vale profound / Is overflowing with the sound.'*

Or is it some more humble lay,
Familiar matter of to-day?—
Some natural sorrow, loss, or pain,
That has been, and may be again?

Whate'er the theme, the Maiden sang
As if her song could have no ending;
I saw her singing at her work,
And o'er the sickle bending;—
I listened motionless and still;
And, as I mounted up the hill,
The music in my heart I bore,
Long after it was heard no more.

ABOVE *Lily of the Valley Island,
Windermere, 1827, a watercolour
by John Harden. Wordsworth had
loved the islands on Windermere
ever since, as a schoolboy, he had
rowed out to them with his
companions: 'the selected bourne /
Was now an Island, musical with
birds / That sang and ceased not;
now a Sister Isle / Beneath the
oaks' umbrageous covert, sown /
With lilies of the valley like a field.'*

One happy result of the Highlands journey was the beginning of a friendship between Wordsworth and Walter Scott, which was to bring pleasure to both. William wrote on his return: 'My sister and I often talk of the happy days which we passed in your Company, such things do not occur often in life. If we live, we shall meet again that is my consolation when I think of these things.'

On another occasion he had declared to the young Thomas De Quincey: 'My friendship it is not in my power to give . . . a sound and healthy friendship is the growth of time and circumstance. It will spring up and thrive like a wild-flower when these favour, and when they do not it is in vain to look for it.' But such was his immediate sense of rapport with Scott that he felt able to conclude his letter: 'Your sincere Friend, for such will I call myself, though slow to use a word of such solemn meaning to any one.'

Earlier in the year Coleridge had made a series of hill walks, the element of danger and the profound solitude bringing release to his spirits. In the depths of the winter he braved the ascent to the top of Kirkstone Pass in a storm, which he described to Tom Wedgwood on 9 January:

> I am no novice in mountain mischiefs, but such a storm as this was I never witnessed, combining the intensity of the cold with the violence of the wind and rain. The rain-drops were pelted or, rather, slung against my face by the gusts, just like splinters of flint, and I felt as if every drop *cut* my flesh. My hands were all shrivelled up like a washerwoman's, and so benumbed that I was obliged to carry my stick under my arm. Oh, it was a wild business! Such hurry-skurry of clouds, such volleys of sound! . . . Just at the brow of the hill I met a man dismounted, who could not sit on horseback. He seemed quite scared by the uproar, and said to me, with much feeling, 'Oh, sir, it is a perilous buffeting, but it is worse for you than for me, for I have it at my back.' However I got safely over, and,

immediately, all was calm and breathless, as if it was some mighty fountain just on the summit of Kirkstone, that shot forth its volcano of air, and precipitated huge streams of invisible lava down the road to Patterdale.

A few days later he wrote of the sense of affinity he felt with the elements when in these solitary heights:

> I never find myself alone within the embracement of rocks and hills, a traveller up an alpine road, but my spirit courses, drives, and eddies, like a Leaf in Autumn: a wild activity, of thoughts, imaginations, feelings, and impulses of motion, rises up from within me—a sort of *bottom-wind*, that blows to no point of the compass, and comes from I know not whence, but agitates the whole of me; my whole Being is filled with waves, as it were, that roll and stumble, one this way, and one that way, like things that have no common master. I think, that my soul must have pre-existed in the body of a Chamois-chaser; . . . In these moments it has been my creed, that Death exists only because Ideas exist that Life is limitless Sensation; that Death is a child of the organic senses, chiefly of the Sight; that Feelings die by flowing into the mould of the Intellect, and becoming Ideas . . . The farther I ascend from animated Nature, from men, and cattle, and the common birds of the woods, and fields, the greater becomes in me the Intensity of the feeling of Life; Life seems to me then a universal spirit, that neither has, nor can have, an opposite.

In September 1803 Robert Southey and his wife Edith, Sara Coleridge's sister, arrived at Greta Hall for a visit, which, as it turned out, was to last for the rest of their lives. Southey was by now the author of a considerable body of work, though none of it was of the calibre of that of Coleridge or Wordsworth. Temperamentally, too, he was very different from them, being reserved, precise and a creature of rigid habit. De Quincey

ABOVE *Kirkstone between Ullswater and Ambleside from John Glover's sketchbook. Kirkstone Pass, high and desolate, was often shrouded in mist. Here Coleridge found himself in a storm: 'The rain-drops were pelted or, rather, slung against my face by the gusts, just like splinters of flint . . . My hands were all shrivelled up like a washerwoman's, and so benumbed that I was obliged to carry my stick under my arm. Oh, it was a wild business! Such hurry-skurry of clouds, such volleys of sound!'*

gave an account of the tortures Southey had to endure over Wordsworth's treatment of the precious volumes in his library:

> Southey had particularly elegant habits (Wordsworth called them finical) in the use of books. Wordsworth, on the other hand, was so negligent and so self-indulgent in the same case, that, as Southey, laughing, expressed it . . . 'To introduce Wordsworth into one's library is like letting a bear into a tulip garden.'

On one occasion Wordsworth took down from De Quincey's shelf an uncut volume of Burke and, seizing on a buttery knife from the tea table, 'tore his way into the heart of the volume with this knife, that left its greasy honours behind it upon every page: and are they not there to this day?'

De Quincey felt that Southey and Wordsworth 'did not cordially like each other. Indeed, it would have been odd if they had. Wordsworth lived in the open air; Southey in his library, which Coleridge used to call his wife.' De Quincey described Southey as 'somewhat taller than Wordsworth' and 'he struck one as a better and lighter figure, to the effect of which his dress contributed; for he wore pretty constantly a short jacket and pantaloons, and had much the air of a Tyrolese mountaineer.' His meticulous turn of mind was shown in a letter he wrote to a friend in Bristol:

RIGHT *View of Keswick from the south window of Southey's study at Greta Hall, a watercolour by Caroline Southey, the writer's second wife. The room commanded spectacular views over Derwentwater to Borrowdale, with Skiddaw in the distance to the right. It housed Southey's extensive library, which Coleridge called 'his wife'.*

> I have a fear upon me least Coleridge should get at my books, and carry any of them off with him: for in the first place he spoils every decent book on which he lays his hands, and in the next place the moment it is in his hands he considers it to all intents and purposes as his own, and makes no scruple of bescrawling it, of giving it away—in short of doing any thing with it, except taking care of it and returning it to its owner.

He went on to issue some detailed instructions:

LEFT *Robert Southey by Henry Edridge, 1804. The portrait dates from a few months after the Southeys arrived at Greta Hall, which they were to share with the Coleridges. Southey is shown surrounded by his books, his greatest treasures. De Quincey said that the poet wore 'pretty constantly a short jacket and pantaloons, and had much the air of a Tyrolese mountaineer.'*

The Batalha book should come in the box of linen which Edith is to have sent by waggon. But tie it and seal it—before you part with it to secure it from possible harm. I dread female fingers, Mrs C's among the numbers. They never can see prints unless they touch them. In this same box or rather in a little hamper with it send me some underground—alias Jerusalem artichokes for setting.

It is easy to mock Southey, but he was a staunch friend and resignedly assumed the care of Mrs Coleridge and her children after Coleridge finally left them. He loved children and like the Pied Piper would take the tribe of Southeys, Coleridges and Wordsworths for long scrambling picnic excursions. Of one such occasion he wrote:

a fine day affects children alike at all seasons as it does the barometer. They live in the present, seldom saddened with any retrospective thoughts, and troubled with no foresight. Three or four days of dull sunless weather had been succeeded by a delicious morning. My young ones were clamorous for a morning's excursion. The glass had risen to a little above change, but their spirits had mounted to the point of settled fair.

Walla Crag was the place selected as the object of this outing with the children:

Away they went to put on coats and clogs, and presently were ready each with her little basket to carry out the luncheon, and bring home such treasures of mosses and lichens as they were sure to find. Off we set; and when I beheld their happiness, and thought how many enjoyments they would have been deprived of, if their lot had fallen in a great city, I blest God who had enabled me to fulfil my heat's desire and live in a country such as Cumberland.

ABOVE *Edith Southey and Sara Coleridge, a drawing by Edward Nash. The cousins (their mothers were sisters) were of an age and were brought up together at Greta Hall. After Coleridge's departure in 1812, Sara had to depend on Southey as a substitute for her father. He proved a kind and generous guardian.*

The perfect eminence was reached, with prospects over Derwentwater, the vale of Keswick and Skiddaw:

This was to be our resting-place, for though the steepest ascent was immediately before us, the greater part of the toil was over. My young companions seated themselves on the fell side, upon some of the larger stones, and there in full enjoyment of air and sunshine opened their baskets and took their noon-day meal, a little before its due time, with appetites which, quickened by exercise, had outstript the hours. My place was on a bough of the ash tree at a little distance, the water flowing at my feet, and the fall just below me. Among all the sights and sounds of Nature there are none which affect me more pleasurably than these.

William Howitt, the author of *Homes and Haunts of the Most Eminent British Poets*, tells an anecdote about him:

Southey's garden, and that of his only neighbour, were merely divided by a hedge. In the garden of the neighbour was sitting once with the neighbour a visitor from a distance, when a deep and mysterious booming, somewhat near, startled the stranger and caused him to listen . . . 'What! have you bitterns here?' 'Bitterns!' replied the host; 'oh no; it is only Southey, humming his verses in the garden walk.'

The spectacle of loving content at Dove Cottage caused Coleridge pangs of envy. He wrote to Thomas Poole, in a tone of irritation, that he saw Wordsworth

more and more benetted in hypochondriacal Fancies, living wholly among *Devotees*—having every the minutest Thing, almost his very Eating and Drinking, done for him by his Sister, or Wife—and I trembled, lest a Film should rise, and thicken on his moral Eye.

LEFT *Derwentwater, Bassenthwaite and Skiddaw from Walla Crag engraved by E. Goodall after William Westall. Robert Southey is shown seated on the branch of an ash tree at Walla Crag, 'the water flowing at my feet, and the fall just below me. Among all the sights and sounds of Nature there are none which affect me more pleasurably than these.' The poet had withdrawn a little distance from the band of children who had coaxed him to take them on a day's expedition and with whom he was a general favourite.*

ABOVE *Edith and Isobel Southey drawn by Edward Nash. The carefree tone of the picture reflects the sense of security Southey gave to all the children in his charge, both his own and Coleridge's.*

The subject of Coleridge's anxiety, however, wrote on the same day, 14 October 1803, of having joined the Westmorland Volunteers, preparations being under way to repel the threatened French invasion. 'At Grasmere, we have turned out almost to a man. We are to go to Ambleside on Sunday to be mustered, and put on, for the first time, our military apparel.' 'Mary and I,' commented Dorothy, 'have no other hope than that they will not be called upon, out of these quiet far-off places, except in case of the French being successful after their landing, and in that case what matter? We may all go together.'

At the end of the year Coleridge arrived at Dove Cottage to say goodbye to his friends before setting off for the Mediterranean in desperate search of physical health and peace of mind. He at once collapsed and remained with the Wordsworths for some weeks. He wrote of this time to his friend Richard Sharp:

> I had only just strength enough to smile gratefully on my kind nurses, who tended me with sister's and mother's love, and often, I well know, wept for me in their sleep, and watched for me even in their dreams. Oh, dear sir! it does a man's heart good, I will not say, to know such a family, but even to know that there *is* such a family.

LEFT AND RIGHT *Pages from the manuscript of* The Prelude *written by the poet in a number of small notebooks, some of which measured only three inches by two.*

The weeks after their friend's eventual departure for London, en route for Malta, were spent by Dorothy and Mary in the laborious and hurried task of transcribing all William's poems for Coleridge to take abroad. (Their handwritten work is to be found at Dove Cottage to this day.) Dorothy described their progress to Coleridge:

> We have transcribed all William's smaller Poems for you, and have begun the Poem on his Life and the Pedlar, but before we send them off we mean to take another Copy for ourselves, for they are scattered about here and there in this book and in

that, one Stanza on one leaf, another on another which makes the transcribing more than twice the trouble, besides the comfort of having them all in one or two nice volumes.

1804 was to be William's most productive year. He worked with great intensity, completing eight books of the second version of *The Prelude*, writing at great speed in small notebooks, some measuring only three inches by two. In the same year he completed the 'Immortality Ode', and composed 'Daffodils' and the 'Ode to Duty'. Dorothy reported that 'He walks out every morning, generally alone, and brings us in a large treat almost every time he goes.' And, later:

> In wet weather he takes out an umbrella, chooses the most sheltered spot, and there walks backwards and forwards, and though the length of his walk be sometimes a quarter or half a mile, he is as fast bound within the chosen limits as if by prison walls.

In March news came that Coleridge had been gravely ill before embarking on his voyage. Wordsworth wrote to him in alarm:

> Your last letter but one informing us of your late attack was the severest shock to me, I think, I have ever received . . . I cannot help saying that I would gladly have given 3 fourths of my possessions for your letter on The Recluse at that time. I cannot say what a load it would be to me, should I survive you and you die without this memorial left behind . . . Heaven bless you for ever and ever. No words can express what I feel at this moment. Farewell farewell farewell.   W.W.

'The Recluse' was to have been Wordsworth's major work, a long philosophical poem on 'Man, Nature and Society', constantly urged upon him by Coleridge. He was never to write it, but its spectre hung uneasily over him for the rest of his life.

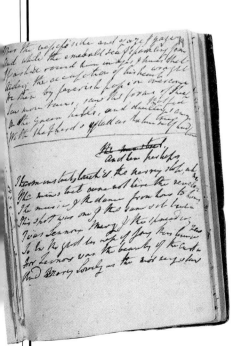

The fame of the 'Lake Poets' was increasing. This imprecise term was being used, rather to Wordsworth's irritation, to refer to himself, Coleridge, Southey and, sometimes, De Quincey. He complained to John Thelwall: 'As to the School about which so much noise (I am told) has been made . . . I do not know what is meant by it nor of whom it consists . . . it is scarcely possible that a greater difference should exist between any set of men or Authors.'

William continued to work steadily, turning some time in March to Dorothy's journal entry of just two years earlier:

> When we were in the woods beyond Gowbarrow park we saw a few daffodils close to the waterside. We fancied that the lake had floated the seeds ashore and that the little colony had so sprung up. But as we went along there were more and yet more and at last under the boughs of the trees, we saw that there was a long belt of them along the shore, about the breadth of a country turnpike road. I never saw daffodils so beautiful they grew among the mossy stones about and about them, some rested their heads upon these stones as on a pillow for weariness and the rest tossed and reeled and danced and seemed as if they verily laughed with the wind that blew upon them over the lake, they looked so gay ever glancing ever changing.

The result was to be the perfect demonstration of William's belief that 'poetry takes its origin from emotion recollected in tranquillity':

> *I wandered lonely as a cloud*
> *That floats on high o'er vales and hills,*
> *When all at once I saw a crowd,*
> *A host, of golden daffodils;*
> *Beside the lake, beneath the trees,*
> *Fluttering and dancing in the breeze.*

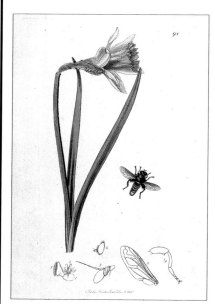

BELOW *No one knows the precise spot where William and Dorothy saw the famous daffodils that inspired 'I wandered lonely as a cloud . . .' It was somewhere between Gowbarrow Park and Patterdale on a walk they took on 15 April 1802.*

RIGHT *Newlands Vale by Rev. Joseph Wilkinson, 1795. Coleridge wrote of his reaction to traversing such a landscape as this, when 'my whole Being is filled with waves, as it were, that roll and stumble, one this way, and one that way, like things that have no common master. I think that my soul must have pre-existed in the body of a Chamois-chaser.'*

Continuous as the stars that shine
And twinkle on the milky way,
They stretched in never-ending line
Along the margin of a bay:
Ten thousand saw I at a glance,
Tossing their heads in sprightly dance.

The waves beside them danced; but they
Out-did the sparkling waves in glee:
A poet could not but be gay,
In such a jocund company:
I gazed—and gazed—but little thought
What wealth the show to me had brought:

For oft, when on my couch I lie
In vacant or in pensive mood,
They flash upon that inward eye
Which is the bliss of solitude;
And then my heart with pleasure fills,
And dances with the daffodils.

RIGHT *The head of Ullswater, Patterdale and the Mountain Helvellyn engraved after Joseph Farington. During their climb of Helvellyn, Wordsworth, Scott and Davy passed the place where a young man had fallen to his death, his body being guarded by his little terrier, who stayed by his master's body for several months. Wordsworth and Scott both wrote poems about this affecting tale, entitled respectively 'Fidelity' and 'Helvellyn'.*

William insisted that 'The best lines in it are by Mary.' Here, as elsewhere in his work, Dorothy's presence is discounted, William choosing to present himself as a solitary observer.

Dora Wordsworth, destined to be her father's darling, was born in August. Dorothy wrote: 'Mrs Coleridge and all her Children were with us when my Sister was taken ill which was at least three weeks before the time expected so we were thrown into a bustle. Mrs C stayed with us till Sunday.'

On Christmas Day 1804 William wrote to his friend and admirer Sir George Beaumont, amateur painter and patron of the arts:

We have lately built in our little rocky orchard a little circular Hut lined with moss like a wren's nest, and coated on the

100

outside with heath that stands most charmingly with several
views . . . of the Lake, the Valley, and the Church.

The moss hut was designed to provide much-needed extra
space, an overflow from the cottage. The Wordsworths loved it
and the building of it epitomized their settled contentment at
the end of a richly productive year.

But on 11 February 1805 news arrived that John Wordsworth
was drowned. His ship, *The Earl of Abergavenny*, a large vessel
of the East India Company's fleet, had sunk off Weymouth Bay

at the outset of a voyage to China. The effect on the Wordsworths was devastating. John had become more and more precious to them during the early months he spent at Dove Cottage, and this first real grief of their adult lives left them bewildered and distraught. William turned at once for comfort to the reserved and aloof Southey:

> If you could bear to come to this house of mourning tomorrow, I should be forever thankful. We weep much to-day, and that relieves us . . . Oh! it makes the heart groan, that, with such a beautiful world as this to live in, and such a soul as that of man's is by nature and gift of God, we should go about on such errands as we do, destroying and laying waste; and ninety-nine of us in a hundred never easy in any road that travels towards peace and quietness! And yet, what virtue and what goodness, what heroism and courage, what triumphs of disinterested love everywhere; and human life, after all, what is it! Surely, this is not to be forever, even in this perishable planet!

To another friend he wrote of John's reserved nature: 'my Father in allusion to this part of his disposition used to call him Ibex, the shyest of all the beasts.' He also spoke of his brother's selfless generosity:

> he encouraged me to persist, and to keep my eye steady on its object. He would work for me . . . and his Sister; and I was to endeavour to do something for the world. A thousand times has he said could I but see you with a green field of your own, and a Cow, and two or three other little comforts, I should be happy!

With John dead and Coleridge far away the six sets of initials carved on the Rock of Names must have seemed a mockery to the mourning Wordsworths.

By June, writing to Lady Beaumont, Dorothy adopted a determinedly hopeful tone:

FAR LEFT AND LEFT *A wren on a mossy branch and a robin. Dorothy wrote to Lady Beaumont on 11 June 1805 of the pleasures of the little moss-lined hut 'like a wren's nest' that she and William had built in the Dove Cottage garden: 'in truth I think it is the sweetest place on Earth—the little wrens often alight upon the thatch and sing their low song.' Robins, too, were frequent visitors to the garden and orchard.*

LEFT *Pencil portrait by Sir George Beaumont, thought to be of his wife. A warm friendship grew up between Lady Beaumont and Dorothy Wordsworth, despite the differences in their circumstances. The two women wrote to one another sympathetically and without restraint. Lady Beaumont was a fervent admirer of William's poetry.*

My dear Friend

It will give you pleasure to hear that I have delayed writing to you in consequence of full employment . . . In the first place we turned to the melancholy garden, and put it into order; the orchard hut, which had remained unfinished since last autumn, we have completed, and our own dwelling-house which had fallen into disorder like other things, we have had set to rights . . . I write to you from the Hut, where we pass all our time except when we are walking—it has been a rainy morning, but we are here sheltered and warm, and in truth I think it is the sweetest place on Earth—the little wrens often alight upon the thatch and sing their low song, but this morning *all* the Birds are rejoicing after the rain.

In the autumn Wordsworth, Walter Scott and Humphry Davy climbed Helvellyn, passing the spot from which a young acquaintance of Wordsworth had fallen to his death. His body had not been found for some months, during all of which time his dog had kept guard over her master. Scott and Wordsworth, unknown to each other and moved by the sad tale, were both engaged in writing poems on the subject.

By now Dorothy's life was becoming increasingly occupied with household cares, although she still managed to compose long letters. At the end of November she wrote:

The Children are now in bed. The evening is very still, and there are no indoor sounds but the ticking of our Family watch which hangs over the chimney-piece under the drawing of the Applethwaite Cottage, and a breathing or a beating of one single irregular Flame in my fire. No one who has not been an Inmate with Children in a *Cottage* can have a notion of the quietness that takes possession of it when they are gone to sleep.

Of the news of Trafalgar she wrote:

RIGHT *The blind fiddler by John Harden, 1807. Perhaps this was the fiddler who visited Dove Cottage on Christmas Day 1805, fiddling in the kitchen for all the neighbourhood children to dance. 'It is a pleasant sound they make with their little pattering feet,' Dorothy wrote to Lady Beaumont.*

We were at Breakfast when Mr Luff's Maid-servant opened the door, and, shewing only her head, with an uncouth stare and a grin of pleasure told us that there had been a great victory, and Lord Nelson was shot. It was a blow. *I* was not collected enough to doubt, and burst into tears; but William would not believe all at once, and forced me to suspend my grief till he had made further inquiries. At the Inn we were told that there were 'great rejoicings at Penrith—all the Bells ringing'. 'Then, I exclaimed, he cannot be dead!' but we soon heard enough to leave us without a doubt, and bitterly did we lament for him and our Country.

On Christmas Day, her thirty-fourth birthday, Dorothy reflected on the Christmas two years before when Coleridge had been with them at Dove Cottage. By now he had left Malta and, she told Lady Beaumont, she dreaded the idea of his voyage:

> Oh my dear Friend, what a fearful thing a windy night is now at our house! I am too often haunted with dreadful images of Shipwrecks and the Sea when I am in bed and hear a stormy wind, and now that we are thinking so much about Coleridge it is worse than ever.

She drew a delightful picture with which to end the year:

> I have been summoned into the kitchen to dance with Johnny and have danced till I am out of breath. According to annual custom, our Grasmere Fiddler is going his rounds, and all the children of the neighbouring houses are assembled in the kitchen to dance. Johnny has long talked of the time when the Fiddler was to come; but he was too shy to dance with any body but me, and though he exhibited very boldly when I was down stairs, I find they cannot persuade him to stir again. It is a pleasant sound they make with their little pattering feet upon the stone floor, half a dozen of them, Boys and Girls.

ABOVE *Two women sewing by candlelight, a pen and wash drawing by John Harden. With a growing family, much of Dorothy and Mary's time was necessarily spent in making clothes, patching and mending, in such scenes as the above. Dorothy was always ready to turn her hand to any household task. In her journal she mentions mattress-making and shoe-making, as well as sewing curtains, and painting and papering rooms.*

DOVE COTTAGE

The Circle Widens

RIGHT *Portrait of Wordsworth by Henry Edridge, painted during the poet's visit to London in the spring of 1806 as he struggled to recover from the grief of his brother's death.*

IN THE SPRING of 1806 Wordsworth paid a visit to London, throwing himself with seeming enthusiasm into a busy social round, of which Southey wrote scathingly: 'Wordsworth flourishes in London, he powders and goes with a cocked hat under his arm to all the great routs. No man is more flattered by the attentions of the great, and no man would be more offended to be told so.' The change was beneficial for him since he had been unwell and lacked the stimulation of new scenes. He now met Charles James Fox, and his portrait was painted by Edridge. At heart he was still grieving for John. On his return to Grasmere, and inspired by Sir George Beaumont's painting of Piel Castle in a storm, which he had seen at the Royal Academy, William wrote a lament for his brother, 'Elegiac Stanzas', which is partly, too, a leave-taking of his own youth, an expression of sadness at the loss of earlier raptures:

FAR RIGHT *Somerset House from the Strand, an aquatint by T. H. Shepherd. Wordsworth enjoyed sightseeing during his visit to London, saw old friends such as the Lambs and made many new acquaintances. He was pleased to be introduced at a ball to Charles James Fox.*

> Ah! then, if mine had been the Painter's hand,
> To express what then I saw; and add the gleam,
> The light that never was, on sea or land,
> The consecration, and the Poet's dream;
>
> I would have planted thee, thou hoary Pile,
> Amid a world how different from this!
> Beside a sea that could not cease to smile;
> On tranquil land, beneath a sky of bliss.
>
> So once it would have been,—'tis so no more;
> I have submitted to a new control:
> A power is gone which nothing can restore;
> A deep distress hath humanised my Soul.

Thomas, the Wordsworths' second son, was born in June; in August Coleridge arrived back in England. But this was not the joyful occasion awaited by his friends: he lingered in the south for ten weeks, and when he did at last reappear his distant manner and gross physical deterioration caused consternation. Dorothy wrote to Catherine Clarkson of meeting him at Kendal:

> We all went thither to him, and never never did I feel such a shock, as at first sight of him . . . He is utterly changed; and yet sometimes, when he was animated in conversation concerning things removed from him, I saw something of his former self; but never when we were alone with him . . . His fatness has quite changed him. It is more like the flesh of a person in a dropsy than one in health; his eyes are lost in it—but why talk of this? you must have seen and felt all.

Coleridge was determined on separation from his wife, and by Christmas he and Hartley were installed with the Wordsworths and Sara Hutchinson at Coleorton, in Leicestershire, in a large farmhouse lent for the winter by the Beaumonts. Dove Cottage was by now uncomfortably cramped and latterly even the smallest bed had to accommodate two people. Dorothy was delighted with the luxury of life at Coleorton as a contrast and detailed for Catherine Clarkson all the joys of plentiful butter, poultry and game, and unlimited coal: 'Sir G has coal pits on his estate, so we have excellent fires.'

At about this time, hurt by Coleridge's manner, Wordsworth wrote 'A Complaint':

> There is a change—and I am poor;
> Your love hath been, nor long ago,
> A fountain at my fond heart's door,
> Whose only business was to flow;
> And flow it did; not taking heed
> Of its own bounty, or my need.

ABOVE *Piel Castle, an engraving after the painting by Sir George Beaumont, the frontispiece illustration to* Poems in Two Volumes *by William Wordsworth, London, 1815, dedicated to Sir George: 'you have peculiar claim—for several of the best pieces were composed under the shade of your own groves, upon the classic ground of Coleorton.' Beaumont's painting, entitled 'Peele Castle in a Storm', inspired Wordsworth to write 'Elegiac Stanzas' for his drowned brother, John Wordsworth.*

RIGHT *Page from Sir George Beaumont's sketchbook of a study of a house among trees, Coleorton, Leicestershire, c. 1810. During the Wordsworths' prolonged stay at Hall Farm, Coleorton, Wordsworth designed a winter garden for the new house Sir George was having built.*

What happy moments did I count!
Blest was I then all bliss above!
Now, for that consecrated fount
Of murmuring, sparkling, living love,
What have I? shall I dare to tell?
A comfortless and hidden well.

A well of love—it may be deep—
I trust it is,—and never dry:
What matter? if the waters sleep
In silence and obscurity.
—Such change, and at the very door
Of my fond heart, hath made me poor.

After Christmas there was a return to some degree of harmony, as William read his completed *Prelude* by candlelight to the little company sitting round the fire: all the signatories, with the sad exception of John Wordsworth, to the Rock of Names. The reading took several consecutive evenings, and its effect, particularly on Coleridge to whom the poem was addressed, must have been overwhelming.

The erstwhile 'archangel, slightly damaged' (as Lamb had described him) listened to the poet he admired above all others reciting his great work, while in the shadows sat the women central to his life, one of whom he agonizingly adored. He lost no time in composing his reply, 'To William Wordsworth: composed on the night after his recitation of a poem on the growth of an individual mind'. It was to be his last important long poem, and it ends on a quiet note:

And when—O Friend! my comforter and guide!
Strong in thyself, and powerful to give strength!—
Thy long sustained Song finally closed,
And thy deep voice had ceased . . .
Scarce conscious, and yet conscious of its close
I sate, my being blended in one thought . . .
And when I rose, I found myself in prayer.

RIGHT *Portrait of Sir George Beaumont by George Dance, painted in 1807 at the time when the Wordsworth family and Coleridge were living in the farmhouse at Coleorton. Beaumont's thoughtful gesture in lending the house gave the Wordsworths a much-needed respite from the cramped conditions at Dove Cottage.*

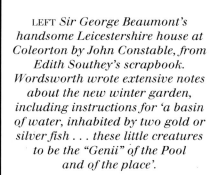

LEFT *Sir George Beaumont's handsome Leicestershire house at Coleorton by John Constable, from Edith Southey's scrapbook. Wordsworth wrote extensive notes about the new winter garden, including instructions for 'a basin of water, inhabited by two gold or silver fish . . . these little creatures to be the "Genii" of the Pool and of the place'.*

The New Year brought hard work for the whole group, which helped to unite them again, as William prepared his new collection, *Poems in Two Volumes*, for publication, the others copying out his manuscripts. But Coleridge soon began to torment himself that Sara loved William more than she did him, even, wildly, that they were already lovers. As his notebooks make clear, he continued to see Wordsworth as an object of veneration, which only made his fantasies the more painful, his jealousy the more acute. That there were still flashes of happiness, however, is made evident in the touching fragment, 'An Angel Visitant', composed at the time:

Within these circling Hollies Woodbine-clad—
Beneath this small blue Roof of vernal Sky—
How warm, how still! tho' tears should dim mine eye,
Yet will my Heart for days continue glad,
For here, my Love, thou art, and here am I!

Poems in Two Volumes appeared in May 1807 to hostile and mocking reviews. William was hurt but managed to write to Lady Beaumont in a lofty tone that disguised his wounds:

> at present let me confine myself to my object, which is to make you, my dear friend, as easy-hearted as myself with respect to these poems. Trouble not yourself upon their present reception; of what moment is that compared with what I trust is their destiny? to console the afflicted; to add sunshine to daylight, by making the happy happier; to teach the young and the gracious of every age, to see, to think and feel; and, therefore, to become more actively and securely virtuous; this is their office, which I trust they will faithfully perform, long after we . . . are mouldered in our graves.

And to Sir George Beaumont he wrote: 'Every great poet is a teacher: I wish either to be considered as a teacher, or as nothing.' This was Wordsworth at his most 'egotistical sublime' (as Keats would later characterize him), with his belief in his vocation apparently absolute and unshaken.

The Wordsworths did not return to Grasmere until the summer of 1807. They felt melancholy: old friends such as Mr Sympson, the Wythbury curate, had died, favourite trees had been felled. But in the autumn there was an important addition to their circle. Thomas De Quincey, best remembered for his *Confessions of an English Opium Eater*, was in that year a youth of twenty-two, tiny, bird-like and brilliant. He had already had a chequered career. His father, a linen merchant, died when he was seven, and his mother treated him coldly and without

RIGHT *Town End, Grasmere, by T. A. Richardson. The cottage consisted of only two downstairs rooms and a back kitchen, a small buttery, cooled by an underground spring, with three bedrooms above, and a tiny unceiled chamber above the buttery. It was known as Town End, Dove Cottage not becoming its familiar name until much later.*

sympathy. He ran away from Manchester Grammar School, where he had shown remarkable ability, and for some time led the life of a penniless vagrant in the London underworld. He was eventually retrieved by his guardians and sent to Worcester College, Oxford.

De Quincey's ambition was to meet Wordsworth, whom he idolized. Twice he travelled to the Lakes in the hope of seeing the poet, only to lose his nerve and turn back at the last moment. Finally, in 1807, he met Coleridge, who entrusted him with the task of escorting Mrs Coleridge and the children from Bristol to Greta Hall. The little party reached Grasmere on 4 November. De Quincey in his *Recollections of the Lakes and the Lake Poets* gave a dramatic account of their arrival, which is also the clearest surviving description of the Dove Cottage household. He and the young Coleridges left the coach and ran down the hill leading to Grasmere,

ABOVE *Grasmere churchyard by William Green. Wordsworth wrote of it in* The Excursion: *'Green is the Churchyard, beautiful and green, / Ridge rising gently by the side of ridge, / A heaving surface, almost wholly free / From interruption of sepulchral stones.' Here he planted yew trees, some of which still remain. The picture shows the river and the old stone bridge.*

> when, all at once, we came at an abrupt turn of the road, in sight of a white cottage, with two solemn yew-trees breaking the glare of its white walls. Had Charlemagne and all his Peerage been behind me, or Caesar and his equipage, or Death on his pale horse, I should have forgotten them at that moment of intense expectation, and of eyes fascinated to what lay before me, or what might in a moment appear . . . I heard a step, a voice, and, like a flash of lightning, I saw the figure emerge of a tallish man, who held out his hand, and saluted me with the most cordial manner, and the warmest expression of friendly welcome that it is possible to imagine.

As Wordsworth turned to greet Mrs Coleridge, De Quincey crossed the threshold. On first leaving the bright daylight he found the interior dark: 'However, I saw sufficiently to be aware of two ladies just entering the room . . . The foremost, a tall young woman, with the most winning expression of benignity upon her features that I had ever beheld.' In spite of her squint, or 'considerable obliquity of vision' as he called it, De Quincey found her beautiful. This was Mary. As for the smaller of the two women:

> 'Her face was of Egyptian brown'; rarely, in a woman of English birth, had I seen a more determinate gipsy tan. Her eyes were not soft, as Mrs Wordsworth's, nor were they fierce or bold; but they were wild and startling, and hurried in their motion. Her manner was warm and even ardent; her sensibility seemed constitutionally deep; and some subtle fire of impassioned intellect apparently burned within her.

This was Dorothy. Next, Wordsworth himself:

> And 'what-like'—to use a Westmoreland, as well as a Scottish expression—'what-like' was Wordsworth? . . . To begin with his figure:—Wordsworth was, upon the whole, not a well-made man. His legs were pointedly condemned by all the female connoisseurs in legs that ever I heard lecture upon that topic . . . undoubtedly they had been serviceable legs beyond the average standard of human requisition; for I calculate, upon good data, that with these identical legs Wordsworth must have traversed a distance of 175 to 180,000 English miles . . . But, useful as they have proved themselves, the Wordsworthian legs were certainly not ornamental . . Meantime, his face—that was one which would have made amends for greater defects of figure; it was certainly the noblest for intellectual effects that, in actual life, I have seen . . . his eyes are not, under any circumstances, bright, lustrous, or piercing; but, after a long day's toil in walking, I have seen them assume an appearance the most solemn and spiritual that it is possible for the human eye to wear.

The Wordsworths immediately took to De Quincey. Dorothy found him to be

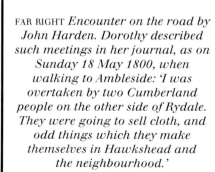

RIGHT *Thomas De Quincey by John Watson Gordon. The young man with his tiny bird-like figure had idolized Wordsworth from afar. Dorothy admired him for his 'loving, gentle and happy' nature. De Quincey is remembered now for his* Confessions of an English Opium Eater.

FAR RIGHT *Encounter on the road by John Harden. Dorothy described such meetings in her journal, as on Sunday 18 May 1800, when walking to Ambleside: 'I was overtaken by two Cumberland people on the other side of Rydale. They were going to sell cloth, and odd things which they make themselves in Hawkshead and the neighbourhood.'*

a remarkable and very interesting young man; very diminutive in person, which, to strangers, makes him appear insignificant; and so modest, and so very shy, that even now I wonder how he had ever the courage to address himself to my brother by letter. I think of this young man with extraordinary pleasure, as he is a remarkable instance of the power of my Brother's poems over a lonely and contemplative mind.

On the third day after their arrival the Wordsworths, De Quincey and the Coleridges made the journey to Greta Hall in a farm cart:

> Such a vehicle I had never in my life seen used for such a purpose; but what was good enough for the Wordsworths was good enough for me . . . Our style of travelling occasioned no astonishment; on the contrary, we met a smiling salutation wherever we appeared—Miss Wordsworth being, as I observed, the person most familiarly known of our party, and the one who took upon herself the whole expenses of the flying colloquies exchanged with stragglers on the road.

De Quincey's first visit to Grasmere was brief, but his popularity was established.

Life in the confines of Dove Cottage had now become unbearable and a larger house in Grasmere, Allan Bank, was reluctantly procured. The move entailed a good deal of expense and Dorothy wrote to William (who was in London trying to help the ailing Coleridge) in an uncharacteristically sharp vein. Wordsworth was unwilling to run the gamut of his persecutors, the reviewers, yet again, and was taking no steps to sell his latest poem, 'The White Doe of Rylstone':

> We are exceedingly concerned, to hear that you, William! have given up all thoughts of publishing your Poem. As to the Outcry against you, I would defy it—what matter, if you get

ABOVE *Engraved frontispiece to* The Miscellaneous Poems of William Wordsworth, *in four volumes, London, 1820, from a painting by Sir George Beaumont. 'During the summer of 1807 the Author visited, for the first time, the beautiful scenery that surrounds Bolton Priory in Yorkshire: and the poem of "The White Doe", founded upon a tradition connected with the place, was composed at the close of the same year.'*

BELOW *Farm cart in Ambleside market place by John Harden. In such a cart did De Quincey, the Coleridges and the Wordsworths visit the Southeys at Greta Hall. De Quincey was taken aback by such a conveyance, 'but what was good enough for the Wordsworths was good enough for me'.*

your 100 guineas into your pocket? . . . without money what *can* we do? New House! new furniture! such a large family! two servants and little Sally! we *cannot* go on so another half-year; and as Sally will not be fit for another place, we must take her back again into the old one, and dismiss one of the Servants, and work the flesh *off our poor bones*. Do, dearest William! do pluck up your Courage—and overcome your disgust to publishing,—It is but a *little trouble*, and all will be over, and we shall be wealthy, and at our ease for one year, at least.

But Wordsworth remained obdurate, publishing no poem for a further seven years. He returned to Grasmere, sad and anxious about Coleridge, and wrote to Sir George Beaumont of a revelatory moment that he had experienced after taking leave of his friend:

I had passed through Temple Bar and by St. Dunstan's, noticing nothing, and entirely occupied with my own thoughts, when, looking up, I saw before me the avenue of Fleet Street, silent, empty, and pure white, with a sprinkling of new-fallen snow, not a cart or carriage to obstruct the view, no noise, only a few soundless and dusky foot-passengers here and there . . . and beyond, towering above it, was the huge and majestic form of St. Paul's, solemnised by a thin veil of falling snow . . . My sorrow was controlled, and my uneasiness of mind—not quieted and relieved altogether—seemed at once to receive the gift of an anchor of security.

At the end of May 1808 the move to Allan Bank was accomplished. It was an emotional moment, the ending of an era. Dorothy wrote sadly: 'the dear cottage! I will not talk of it. Today the loveliness of the outside, the laburnums being in the freshness of their beauty, made me quite sad—and all within, how desolate!'

ABOVE *Laburnum by William Curtis, 1792. The Wordsworths moved from Dove Cottage at the end of May 1808. Dorothy wrote of the pain of leaving the 'dear cottage' and the garden she had created.*

ALLAN BANK

$\mathcal{T}$HE $\mathcal{B}$REACH
WITH $\mathcal{C}$OLERIDGE $\mathcal{B}$EGINS

EARLY IN 1805 Wordsworth had written in indignation to Richard Sharp, a London acquaintance, deploring what he saw as the ruination of the unspoilt beauty of the Vale by the prominent siting of a large new house:

> A wretched creature, wretched in name and nature, of the name of *Crump*, goaded on by his still more wretched wife . . . has at last begun to put his long impending threats in execution; and when you next enter the sweet paradise of Grasmere you will see staring you in the face, upon that beautiful ridge that elbows out into the vale, (behind the church, and towering far above its steeple), a temple of abomination, in which are to be enshrined Mr. and Mrs. Crump.

Three years later he became the first tenant of Allan Bank, that same temple of abomination. Dorothy wrote on arrival to Catherine Clarkson:

> We are now, however, tolerably settled; though there is much to do for Henry and me, who are the only able-bodied people in the house except the servant and *William*, who you know is not expected to do anything. Henry is the most useful creature in the world, and, being very poor, we are determined to make the Carpets and do everything ourselves, for he is as good as a tailor, and at the same time a very pleasant companion, and fellow-labourer.

RIGHT *Brathay Bridge by P. H. de Loutherbourg, 1805. Wordsworth remarked on 'the great number of bridges over the brooks and torrents, and the daring and graceful neglect of danger or accommodation with which so many of them are constructed'. He praised 'the proportion between the span and elevation of the arch, the lightness of the parapet, and the graceful manner in which its curve follows faithfully that of the arch'.*

Henry Hutchinson, a sailor, was Mary's brother, and his presence was fortunate since Sara Hutchinson was ill with a pulmonary complaint and Mary was again pregnant. 'Sara sews a little, but we suffer nothing that can fatigue her, and Dearest Mary sprained her right arm three weeks ago and cannot yet use it even to write a letter.' But in spite of all the hard work Dorothy was determined to make the best of things:

> Sara and I have a delicious view from our several room windows . . . It is a soothing scene, and I trust you will one day behold it, and sit with me in this my little castle, where I now write. We already feel the comfort of having each a room of our own, and begin to love them.

Soon, however, the family were to discover the drawbacks of life in the new house. Every chimney smoked and nothing seemed to effect a cure. Dorothy began to despair:

> Dishes are washed, and no sooner set into the pantry than they are covered with smoke. Chairs, carpets, the painted ledges of the rooms, all are ready for the reception of soot and smoke, requiring endless cleaning, and are never clean . . . In fact we have seldom an hour's leisure (either Mary or I) till after 7 o'clock (when the children go to bed), for all the time that we have for sitting still in the course of the day we are obliged to employ in scouring.

To Jane Marshall she wrote: 'There was one stormy day in which we could have no fire but in my Brother's Study—and that chimney smoked so much that we were obliged to go to bed with the Baby in the middle of the day to keep it warm.'

The household by now was large: the new baby, Catharine, had been born on 6 September, Coleridge having moved in the previous week. At one point even the estranged Mrs Coleridge came to stay too, bringing her little daughter with her; and the

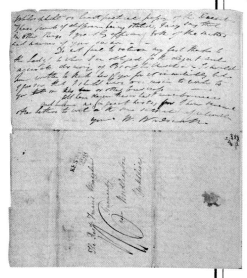

RIGHT *The prospectus for* The Friend *and the periodical's front cover. The launching of Coleridge's 'weekly essay' threw the inhabitants of Allan Bank into a fever of activity. Wordsworth wrote on the reverse of the prospectus (as shown above) to his and Coleridge's old friend, the liberal cleric Francis Wrangham. The first issue appeared on 1 June 1809 after months of exhausting preparation. For the length of its twenty-seven issues it was edited and largely written by Coleridge, with occasional contributions from Wordsworth and others.*

Coleridge boys, at school in Ambleside, spent their weekends at Allan Bank. The household often amounted to fifteen people: more a community than a family.

In November 1808 De Quincey arrived and was such a success with the children that he was asked to remain, a welcome addition to the party. 'We feel often,' Dorothy wrote, 'as if he were one of the family—he is loving, gentle, and happy . . . there is a sweetness in his looks, especially about the eyes, which soon overcomes the oddness of your first feeling at the sight of so very little a man.'

The two poets, meanwhile, disregarding the smoke, were absorbed in their work. In one room Coleridge dictated to Sara,

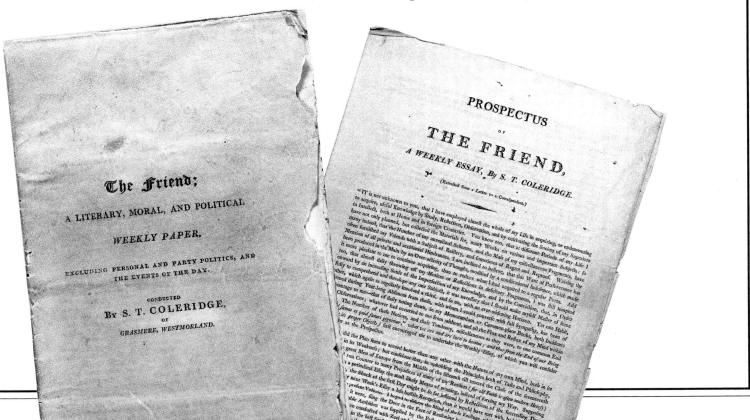

still convalescent from her illness, and surely most vulnerable to the tainted atmosphere. Coleridge was planning his periodical, *The Friend*, writing prospectuses, dashing off essays, requesting contributions. In another room Wordsworth dictated his impassioned political pamphlet on the Convention of Cintra to Mary. This was a protest against what was widely seen as an inept treaty between the defeated French army and the British, who were accused of treachery to their allies, the Spanish and the Portuguese. The issue became an obsession with Wordsworth. The pamphlet was published the following May and Wordsworth feared it could be actionable. Dorothy had reported to De Quincey: 'William still continues to haunt himself with fancies about Newgate and Dorchester or some other gaol, but as his mind clings to the gloomy, Newgate is his favourite theme.'

At the beginning of June, and after hectic months of work, the first number of *The Friend* appeared. It was to run for twenty-seven issues.

A Guide to the Lakes belongs to this time. It was not a guide in the usual sense but rather an evocation of place, drawing upon Wordsworth's intimate and sympathetic knowledge of the mountains and valleys, and setting out his strongly held views on the preservation of their beauty. Houses (such as Allan Bank) must not form a harsh contrast to their surroundings but blend harmoniously; planting, if done at all, must make use of indigenous trees and shrubs; the eye of the beholder must not fall on any anachronism but all must be appropriate and serene. It was a charming exposition of Romantic landscape values and immensely popular, both then and later.

William had taken a further lease of Dove Cottage for De Quincey, and Dorothy busied herself with the necessary decorating and furnishing. To be back in her own moss hut brought a refreshment of spirit after the miseries of the winter months. She wrote frequently to De Quincey, who was in London, detailing the work in progress (including the making of

ABOVE *Manuscript of a letter from De Quincey to Wordsworth's son John, with a drawing of a child's carriage, March 1809. All the Wordsworth children loved De Quincey, who was a great provider of palatable instruction mixed with delightful treats. His diminutive frame helped to give the children a sense of affinity with him.*

RIGHT *View of Buttermere with cattle beside the Fish Inn and a chapel beyond by Julius Caesar Ibbetson, 1813. The Fish Inn was notorious as the home of the beautiful Mary Robinson, the Maid of Buttermere. She was seduced, bigamously married and deserted by a confidence trickster, who was later hanged for forgery. The Maid's story aroused much public sympathy (and curiosity). Wordsworth wrote of her in* The Prelude *and Coleridge visited her deceiver in the condemned cell at Carlisle, afterwards sending an account of the case to* The Morning Post.

elaborate bookshelves and mahogany furniture, which she thought an extravagance) and reminding him to bring a store of tea and some silver spoons. In the autumn he returned to Grasmere and celebrated with a New Year firework party for all the children of the Vale.

During the following winter Coleridge worked at great speed, sometimes producing complete numbers of *The Friend* in the space of two days. But in March the venture was abandoned. Dorothy, once his greatest champion, now began to feel exasperated with her trying guest. 'We have no hope of him,' she wrote to Catherine Clarkson:

> He lies in bed, always till after 12 o'clock, sometimes much later; and never walks out . . . He never leaves his own parlour, except at dinner and tea, and sometimes supper, and then he always seems impatient to get back to his solitude . . . Sometimes he does not speak a word.

She may not have been aware that he was struggling unsuccessfully to escape from the miseries of his addiction to opium and brandy. In March, Sara Hutchinson, worn out by Coleridge's emotional demands, which had brought her recurring nervous disorders and feelings of disgust at his physical presence, left Allan Bank. She returned as a permanent member of the Wordsworth household only after Coleridge's final departure. He left for Keswick in May 1810; at the end of the month Mary gave birth to her last child, another William Wordsworth.

Wordsworth, like the rest of his family, welcomed De Quincey's company. The latter tells of night walks together, sometimes to meet the carrier who was bringing their copy of *The Courier*:

> Wordsworth and I would walk off to meet him about midnight,
> to a distance of three or four miles . . . At intervals,

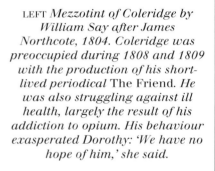

LEFT *Mezzotint of Coleridge by William Say after James Northcote, 1804. Coleridge was preoccupied during 1808 and 1809 with the production of his short-lived periodical* The Friend. *He was also struggling against ill health, largely the result of his addiction to opium. His behaviour exasperated Dorothy: 'We have no hope of him,' she said.*

Wordsworth had stretched himself at length on the high road, applying his ear to the ground, so as to catch any sound of wheels that might be groaning along at a distance. Once, when he was slowly rising from this effort, his eye caught a bright star that was glittering between the brow of Seat Sandal and of the mighty Helvellyn. He gazed upon it for a minute or so.

Recovering himself, Wordsworth explained his momentary abstraction to his companion:

Just now my ear was placed upon the stretch, in order to catch any sound of wheels . . . at the very instant when the organs of attention were all at once relaxing from their tension, the bright star hanging in the air above those outlines of massy blackness fell suddenly upon my eye, and penetrated my capacity of apprehension with a pathos and a sense of the infinite, that would not have arrested me under other circumstances.

The two of them once called in on a friendly stranger, a 'man-mountain'. De Quincey again passed his house at night:

Nine o'clock it was—and deadly cold as ever March night was made by the keenest of black frosts, and by the bitterest of north winds—when I drew towards the gate of our huge and hospitable friend . . . A little garden there was before the house, and in the centre of this garden was placed an arm-chair, upon which arm-chair was sitting composedly—but I rubbed my eyes, doubting the very evidence of my own eye-sight—a or *the* huge man in his shirt-sleeves; yes, positively not sunning but *mooning* himself—apricating himself in the occasional moonbeams; and, as if simple star-gazing from a sedentary station were not sufficient on such a night, absolutely pursuing his astrological studies, I repeat, in his shirt-sleeves!

Leaving Mary with her new baby, William and Dorothy paid a round of visits in the summer of 1810, at first together, later separating. During this two-month period William and Mary wrote a series of delightful letters to one another, both tender and intimate. This was only the second time in their marriage that they had been separated for any significant length of time and they found the experience painful. William wrote from Radnorshire on Sunday 22 July:

> Our Friends here look forward to a repetition of this visit next year; but I cannot think of any thing of the kind; nor will I ever, except from a principle of duty, part from you again, to stay any where more than one week. I cannot bear it.

Mary's reply opens:

> O My William! it is not in my power to tell thee how I have been affected by this dearest of all letters—it was so unexpected—so new a thing to see the breathing of thy inmost heart upon paper that I was quite overpowered . . . I have brought my paper, after having laid my baby upon thy sacred pillow, into my own, into *thy* own room—and write from Sara's little Table, retired from the window which looks upon the lasses strewing out the hay in an uncertain Sun.

On 11 August William declared: 'O Mary I love you with a passion of love which grows till I tremble to think of its strength.' On 14 August Mary wrote again:

> My dearest love . . . O what would not I give to see thee for one moment!—Lloyd has pleased me by telling me, what I rather wish I had heard from some one more to be depended upon, that he never 'saw me look so well in his life' . . . To be sure I had popped on my laced cap before I went down to them which might make a change in my appearance or I have

ABOVE *Manuscript of a letter from Mary Wordsworth to William, 15 August 1810, one of a series she wrote to her husband during his two-month absence. The correspondence shows the couple's devotion to one another, and how passionately they resented their short separation.*

RIGHT *Bassenthwaite Church. Mary wrote to William: 'I believe the fine folks at the church style fancy as I pass with the Baby in my Arms that I am a shabby Nurse Maid of the great house.' William was incensed at such a misconception.*

myself fancied I was become like nobody in my looks and appearance—I believe the fine folks at the church style fancy as I pass with the Baby in my Arms that I am a shabby Nurse Maid of the great house—for they brush or gallop past me without ever such a thought seeming to enter their head as, that I am a Gentleman's wife—Certainly my *dress* does not entitle me to much respect.

Charles Lloyd, mentioned in the letter, was a minor poet who lived at Old Brathay, not far from the Wordsworths. He was

subject to epileptic fits and irrational behaviour, which may account for Mary's doubts about the reliability of his opinion.

From William's letter of 19 August:

> My darling, I hope, we shall not part again speedily! What happiness did that part of thy Letter give me in which thou speaks of the Compliments received upon thy good looks—Let me here exact a promise from thee, that when thou hast reason to expect me, thou wilt not fail to put on that Cap in which by thy own confession thou lookest best . . . And here let me not forget to add that I will bring thee a Bonnet from Liverpool, a Gypsey one Joanna recommends, and such it shall be if I can please myself . . . By the bye, who are the fine folks at the Church stile?—who presume to look insolently upon thee with our little William in thy arms?

Finally, Mary wrote to William on 24 August, anticipating the joys of being reunited so that they could go together on 'long half-day rambles about, or out of the Vale'. The baby would be no impediment:

> I carry this little fellow about with me just as we used to do John, and with as much or more ease and he is a child that you may do what you please with.—such a Sleeper! and such a Thriver!—He is to be cut for the small pox on Sunday . . . The children have all been about me during breakfast, nursing a dying chicken again—You would have been entertained to have heard the wishes they uttered for Hartleys arrival, whom they look upon to be infallible—one having recovered under his direction last week—but he is come and this poor thing will die in spite of him—to be sure he told them upon learning that the Cock had pecked it—that he was not a 'proficient in cases of surgery—it was only internal diseases that he understood'—he is wonderfully good natured with them for they almost tease his life out.

BELOW *Letter from Mary Wordsworth to her husband, 15 August 1810. Mary, hitherto a shadowy figure, is shown in these letters, recently discovered, to have had a passionate love for William and strong views of her own.*

She continues lovingly that he must stay away longer if he or others wish it, 'for I will prepare myself to expect such a thing'. She ends: 'Farewell my best beloved, above all be good to thyself—and this is the best thou canst do for us all who love thee.'

Shortly after the traveller's return in September, his old friend Basil Montagu arrived to stay at Dove Cottage, remaining for a month. During that time Montagu, shocked by Coleridge's condition, offered to take him to recuperate in his house in London. Coleridge accepted the offer, but Wordsworth privately warned Montagu against the plan, explaining to him some of the disadvantages of having Coleridge as a guest. Montagu ignored the advice and on the journey south he repeated to Coleridge all that Wordsworth had said, possibly with exaggeration or embellishment. Coleridge was deeply offended, but the Wordsworths remained for some months in ignorance of the consequent storm about to break over their heads.

For the time being the family had other preoccupations: the children had whooping cough and Catharine had been dangerously ill. William, Mary and Dorothy took them for a change of air to Little Langdale to stay with the parents of their young servant, Sarah Youdell. Dorothy described their holiday to Catherine Clarkson:

> It is as poor a cottage as ever you saw, standing upon a hill-top overlooking little Langdale, Tilberthwaite, Colwith, and the vale of Brathay; warm because it fronts the south, and sheltered behind by crags . . . at the door choose to the right or to the left and you have mountains, hamlets, woods, cottages, and rocks. The weather was heavenly, when we were there, and the first morning we sat in hot sunshine on a crag, twenty yards from the door, while William read part of the fifth Book of *Paradise Lost* to us. He read *The Morning Hymn*, while a stream of white vapour, which covered the valley of Brathay, ascended slowly and by degrees melted away. It seemed as if we had never before felt deeply the power of the Poet.

LEFT *Little Langdale Water. Looking down from Sarah Youdell's cottage above Little Langdale, Dorothy described William reading 'The Morning Hymn' from* Paradise Lost *to his family, 'while a stream of white vapour, which covered the valley of Brathay, ascended slowly and by degrees melted away'.*

GRASMERE RECTORY

A Year of Tragedies

I N JUNE 1811, the lease of Allan Bank having come to an end, the Wordsworths moved to Grasmere Rectory. The house was low-lying, damp, dark and lacking in privacy. It had little to recommend it and was to be the scene of the most tragic year of the Wordsworths' lives.

Word had by now reached Grasmere that Coleridge found himself 'cruelly injured' over Wordsworth's supposed slights. In February 1812, on his way to Keswick, he drove straight past the Wordsworths' house, the two little boys, Hartley and Derwent, in silent tears of consternation and disappointment. He left Keswick at the end of March without having seen his old friends or replied to Wordsworth's anxious letters.

In April, having heard that Coleridge was speaking of him as his 'bitterest calumniator', Wordsworth went to London to try to effect a reconciliation. Half literary London seems to have joined in the tricky negotiations. Henry Crabb Robinson the diarist, Charles Lamb, the poet Samuel Rogers and Coleridge's benefactor Josiah Wedgwood, offered themselves as intermediaries. Finally a lukewarm truce was achieved, Coleridge telling Crabb Robinson 'in a half whisper' that he was prepared to accept Wordsworth's version of the case. He later wrote to Thomas Poole, quoting aptly from his 'Christabel':

Alas! they had been Friends in Youth!
But whisp'ring Tongues can poison Truth;
And Constancy lives in Realms above;
And Life is thorny; and Youth is vain;
And to be wroth with one we love
Doth work, like Madness, in the Brain!

ABOVE *Portrait of Charles Lamb by William Hazlitt, 1804. Lamb, a loyal friend to both Wordsworth and Coleridge, tried anxiously to reconcile the poets during their unhappy quarrel. It was never fully resolved.*

RIGHT *Hereford, a distant view, drawn and engraved by Copley Fielding. In April 1812 Mary took her little son Thomas on a visit to her brother's farm Hindwell, near Hereford. Mary delighted in the sightseeing. She wrote to William: 'Oh with what a fervent heart did I greet the River Wye for thy sake and for its own loveliness!'*

He then went on to add:

> You perhaps may likewise have heard (*in the Whispering Gallery of the World*) of the year-long difference between me and Wordsworth (compared with the sufferings of which all the former afflictions of my life were less than flea-bites), occasioned in *great part* by the wicked folly of the arch-fool Montagu.
>
> A reconciliation has taken place, but the *feeling*, which I had previous to that moment when the (three-fourth) calumny burst, like a thunderstorm from a blue sky, on my soul, after fifteen years of such religious, almost superstitious idolatry and self-sacrifice. Oh, no! no! that, I fear, never can return.

BELOW *Portrait of Samuel Rogers by Sir Thomas Lawrence. Rogers, an accomplished poet, with a sharp and sarcastic turn of mind, visited the Wordsworths in the Lakes. Later, he good-naturedly lent Wordsworth his court dress when, as Laureate, the latter had to appear at the Queen's ball, complete with wig and sword.*

BELOW *John Bellingham, notorious as the murderer of Spencer Perceval, the Prime Minister, in the Lobby of the House of Commons. An engraving of 1812.*

The whole wretched affair was the culmination of the rift that had been gradually widening between the two poets. The Arcadian days when Coleridge is said to have declared Wordsworth, Dorothy and himself to be 'three people but one soul' were long past. He never returned to Grasmere.

During William's stay in London, Mary, taking little Thomas with her, visited her brother Tom near Hereford. William, harassed by the Coleridge affair, longed to be with her, exploring the river Wye and perhaps revisiting Tintern Abbey: 'How I long my darling to see thy face again; and Little Thomas I am happy that his good Friends are pleased with him. How rich should I be if I had nobody in the world to love but you two.'

On 11 May Spencer Perceval, the Prime Minister, was assassinated in the Lobby of the House of Commons. He was shot dead by a man named Bellingham, formerly a merchant of Liverpool. 'The Assassin has not been executed in Palace Yard as was first proposed,' wrote William, 'had that been the place I should this morning have been a Spectator in safety, from the top of Westminster Abbey; but he suffered before Newgate; and I did not think myself justified, for the sake of curiosity in running any risk.' William's caution was justifiable: riots were

RIGHT *While in London, Wordsworth had it in mind to watch John Bellingham's execution from the top of Westminster Abbey, but in fact the murderer 'suffered before Newgate'.*

RIGHT *Lord Byron after C. H. Harlow. Wordsworth met Byron in London. The latter had written a satire on the Lake Poets, Wordsworth told Mary, 'but these are little thought of'.*

anticipated and the country was in a ferment of unrest. He told of making a new acquaintance:

> This Letter will be franked by Lord Byron, a Man who is now the rage in London, in consequence of his Late Poem Childe Haroldes pilgrimage. He wrote a satire some time since in which Coleridge and I were abused, but these are little thought of; and the other day I met him here.

Coleridge had been giving a series of public lectures on Shakespeare, some brilliant, others disconcertingly incoherent:

> I do not think, they will bring him much profit. He has a world of bitter enemies, and is deplorably unpopular.—Besides people of rank are very shabby for the most part, and will never pay down their five shillings when they can avoid it.

Mary replied on 23 May, giving a report on little Thomas:

I wish you could but see how busy little Totts is riding backwards and forwards all day with the dung cart—this will do him good—he is too fond of housestaying . . . but he is a sweet Boy and I think this journey will have made impressions upon him which will be lasting, and he will be better for it hereafter.

She continued with a shiver of premonition:

I have had no intelligence from Grasmere since the letter which you sent to me and I begin, not to be uneasy about them, but uneasy with myself that I do not hear again—it is a fortnight since that letter was written which seems a long time not to know what has past at home. Those 2 littlest Darlings, how my heart does beat when I think about them.

On 3 June came a passionate outburst from William:

Oh my beloved . . . speak for me to thyself, find the evidence of what is passing within me in *thy* heart, in thy mind, in thy steps as they touch the green grass, in thy limbs as they are stretched upon the soft earth . . . find it in thy lips themselves, and such kisses as I often give to the empty air, and in the aching of thy bosom, and let a voice speak for me in every thing within thee and without thee.

But, as he was writing this lyric declaration of continuing love, his four-year-old daughter Catharine lay dead. It fell to Dorothy to break the terrible news.

My dearest Brother –
Sara and John and William and I are all in perfect health—but poor Catharine died this morning at $\frac{1}{4}$ past 5 o'clock. She had been even better and more chearful than usual all yesterday . . .
Mr Scambler has promised us to write to you by this same

ABOVE LEFT AND RIGHT *Miniatures thought to be of Wordsworth's children Thomas and Catharine, c. 1811. The portraits were kept with William and Mary's love letters, which only came to light in 1977.*

post, with an account of her illness . . . Upon most mature deliberation we have concluded it best not to write to Mary—It would be impossible for her to be here at the Funeral; and we think that she will be better able to stand the shock when it is communicated by you . . . We purpose burying the beloved Girl on Monday. This we do for the best—and we hope you will both be satisfied.

Mary later wrote across the top of one of her happy letters to William: 'Our Child had been 4 days dead!'

Dorothy had also to break the news to De Quincey, whose especial treasure Catharine had been. He was devastated: 'I returned hastily to Grasmere,' he later recalled, 'stretched myself every night, for more than two months running, upon

LEFT *Dame school, Elterwater, by John Harden. Wordsworth taught for a while in 1811 in such a school. It was housed in the tiny building, now the gingerbread shop, next to the churchyard in Grasmere, where his son John, disappointingly slow to learn, was a pupil.*

her grave; in fact, often passed the night upon her grave . . . in mere intensity of sick, frantic yearning after neighbourhood to the darling of my heart.'

Catharine had possessed some elfin or comic quality that found an echo in De Quincey. He dwelt on his last meeting with her when he had been setting off for London:

> The last words which she said to me . . . I think were these: the children were speaking to me all at once, and I was saying one thing to one and another to another; and she, who could not speak loud enough to overpower the other voices, had got up on a chair by which I was standing; and putting her hand upon my mouth she said with her sweet importunateness of voice and gesture—Kinsey—Kinsey; what a-bring Katy from London? . . . This was the last time that I heard her sweet voice.

The tragedies of 1812 were not yet complete: on 1 December Thomas (the 'little Totts' of Mary's letter) died of pneumonia following measles. He was six years old, and everyone's darling, sweet-natured and loving. Once again, as on the death of John in 1805, Wordsworth turned to Southey:

> He did not appear to suffer much in body, but I fear something in mind as he was of an age to have thought much upon death a subject to which his mind was daily led by the grave of his Sister . . . For myself dear Southey I dare not say in what state of mind I am; I loved the Boy with the utmost love of which my soul is capable, and he is taken from me . . . O Southey feel for me!

Wordsworth informed Coleridge of Thomas's death, imploring him to write, which he duly did, in almost his old affectionate tone. But although he promised to visit the prostrated Wordsworths, he never came.

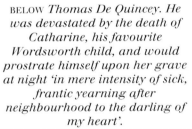

BELOW *Thomas De Quincey. He was devastated by the death of Catharine, his favourite Wordsworth child, and would prostrate himself upon her grave at night 'in mere intensity of sick, frantic yearning after neighbourhood to the darling of my heart'.*

The cruel loss of two children in such a brief space of time gave rise to anxiety for Mary, who became painfully thin and listless, and subject to uncontrollable bouts of weeping. It was clear that the family must leave the Rectory as soon as it could be arranged. 'We are determined upon quitting Grasmere,' wrote Dorothy,

> wherever we look we are reminded of some pretty action of those innocent Children—especially Thomas whose life latterly has been connected with the church-yard in the most affecting manner—there he played daily amongst his schoolfellows, and daily tripped through it to school, a place which was his pride and delight.

The search for a house began again, and soon negotiations were under way to acquire the lease of Rydal Mount, an imposing house a few miles from Grasmere.

At some point during the next year William wrote 'Surprised by Joy', the anguished sonnet which he later said was inspired by Catharine's death:

LEFT *Drawing by Dora Wordsworth of the house and garden of Rydal Mount, c. 1830. Here the Wordsworths lived, driven from Grasmere Rectory by its tragic associations, from 1813 until the end of their lives.*

> *Surprised by joy—impatient as the Wind*
> *I turned to share the transport—Oh! with whom*
> *But Thee, deep buried in the silent tomb,*
> *That spot which no vicissitude can find?*
> *Love, faithful love, recalled thee to my mind—*
> *But how could I forget thee? Through what power,*
> *Even for the least division of an hour,*
> *Have I been so beguiled as to be blind*
> *To my most grievous loss!—That thought's return*
> *Was the worst pang that sorrow ever bore,*
> *Save one, one only, when I stood forlorn,*
> *Knowing my heart's best treasure was no more;*
> *That neither present time, nor years unborn*
> *Could to my sight that heavenly face restore.*

RYDAL MOUNT

*S*AGE OF THE *L*AKES

'**M**Y DEAR FRIEND,' wrote Dorothy to Jane Marshall on 2 May 1813, the day after leaving Grasmere, 'When I tell you that we removed yesterday, you will not wonder, that I write a short note.' However great the emotional and domestic turmoil, her characteristic first instinct was to unburden herself on paper to a sympathetic friend.

> We are all well, though some of us, especially my Sister, jaded with our fatigues. The weather is delightful, and the place a paradise; but my inner thoughts will go back to Grasmere. I was the last person who left the House yesterday evening. It seemed as quiet as the grave; and the very church-yard where our darlings lie, when I gave a last look upon it [seemed] to chear my thoughts.

Rydal Mount, the 'paradise' in question, a handsome house standing on a hillside overlooking Rydal Water and on beyond to Silver How mountain, was to be the Wordsworths' home for the rest of their lives. William, through the influence of Lord Lonsdale, had obtained a government appointment as Distributor of Stamps for Westmorland and the Penrith District of Cumberland. The work was no sinecure and the salary much less than had at first been hoped; but it made the move to a more expensive house feasible, although it did not allow for any relaxation in the family's frugal habits. Most of the poet's friends rejoiced for him, but he was criticized by others. The painter Benjamin Robert Haydon, for example, felt that 'a man's liberty is gone the moment he becomes an official.' The increasing expenses of Wordsworth's family left him, in fact, with little alternative.

ABOVE *Wordsworth's stamp office, Ambleside, by John Harden. In 1813 Wordsworth was appointed Distributor of Stamps for Westmorland and the Penrith District of Cumberland, and was responsible for the issue of taxed stamped paper used in legal transactions.*

RIGHT *Ullswater by Joseph Wright of Derby. The painting, with its mysterious colouring, uncannily evokes that sense of strange presences permeating Wordsworth's much earlier account of stealing a boat, an escapade of his boyhood.*

The move marked a turning-point in the poet's life: behind him lay youth, hope and freedom, and ahead responsibility, increasing fame and literary influence. For the women its immediate effect was to help to distract their thoughts from the tragedies of 1812 as they struggled with the strenuous business of moving house. By September 1813 Dorothy was able to write cheerfully to Catherine Clarkson of the purchase of new carpets. On arrival at Dove Cottage twelve years before they had made their own.

> We are going to have a *Turkey*!!! carpet—in the dining-room, and a Brussels in William's study. You stare, and the simplicity of the dear Town End Cottage comes before your eyes, and you are tempted to say, 'Are they changed, are they setting up for fine Folks' . . . Tom Monkhouse has been the purchaser of these sumptuous wares, and got them at the cheapest hand.

As they had at Dove Cottage, the Wordsworths set to work at once in the garden. 'We are all gardeners,' Dorothy wrote; and the digging, planting and designing helped to reassure them that they themselves were putting down lasting roots. Auction sales produced bargains in the way of necessary furnishings, and Dorothy described one particularly successful occasion: 'We stayed the sale out to the very last and the beds were sold by candle-light and all walked home in the bright moonshine, I with a water decanter and Glass in my hand and William and Mary with a large looking glass—oval with a gilt frame.'

Although the Wordsworths never exactly became 'fine folks', the balance of their lives did change. William dedicated his long poem *The Excursion* to Lord Lonsdale as a tribute to his patron; and there were enjoyable visits to Lonsdale's Lowther Castle, where the poet met such grandees as the Duchess of Richmond, who in 1815 would give the renowned Brussels ball on the eve of the Battle of Waterloo. Later on there was even a ball at Rydal Mount.

ABOVE *Wax medallion of Robert Southey at the time he reluctantly accepted the Poet Laureateship. He stipulated that he should not be expected 'to write odes as boys write exercises'.*

William made more frequent visits to London, meeting many of the prominent figures of the day and being increasingly lionized himself; and from time to time he enjoyed the stimulation of Continental tours. Rydal Mount was often full of guests and, as time went on and William's fame grew, there was a constant stream of visitors to the Lakes hoping to make the acquaintance of the great poet and his family.

The three remaining Wordsworth children were anxiously watched over by their parents and aunt, understandably nervous about their health. Wordsworth adored and petted the little William, rather to Dorothy's disapproval, and she complained that the child was in danger of becoming spoilt; John was slow at his books; Dora lacked concentration. In fact these children, unlike the young Coleridges, seem to have been disappointingly ordinary.

In November 1813 Southey became Poet Laureate, having first stipulated that he would not 'write odes as boys write exercises at stated times and upon stated subjects'. Mrs Southey received a rhyme to commemorate her husband's elevation:

I have something to tell you which you will not be sorry at.
Tis that I am sworn into the office of Laureat.
The oath which I took, there could be nothing wrong in.
Twas to do all the duties to the dignity belonging.
Keep this I charge you as a precious gem.
For this is the Laureats first poemm.

The little cousins Edith Southey and Sara Coleridge made a laurel wreath to crown the poet on his return to Greta Hall.

Southey brought back good news of Coleridge from London: 'Coleridge *has* left off laudanum and God grant that he may never return to it. When last he took it, it was in the quantity of two quarts a week, the cost of which is five pounds, and sometimes he swallowed a pint a day.' Coleridge, having removed himself from the mischief-making Montagus, had taken refuge

ABOVE *Room at Rydal Mount, an engraving after William Westall, 1840. The poet's study. A servant is said to have shown the room to a stranger, remarking that it was Wordsworth's library where he kept his books, 'but his study is out of doors'.*

ABOVE *Engraving after Daniel Maclise entitled 'Wm. Wordsworth, author of "The Excursion"', 1832. Wordsworth's long poem* The Excursion *was published in 1814 in a luxurious edition with a dedicatory sonnet to Lord Lonsdale. The influential* Edinburgh Review's *attack on the volume came as a blow to the poet, who was provoked into making an injudicious reply.*

with John Morgan and his wife, kind and long-suffering friends. Mrs Morgan told Southey that on giving up the laudanum 'for two or three days and nights he suffered dreadfully, falling asleep every minute and waking almost instantly with violent screams.'

The Coleridge children's upbringing devolved almost entirely upon Southey, although Wordsworth always interested himself in Hartley's career, helping to raise funds to enable him to go up to Merton College, Oxford, in 1815. Hartley never fulfilled the promise of his 'exquisitely wild' childhood, when he had so entranced his father. He wrote poems, taught a little, became more and more eccentric and drank a good deal. William remained fond of him, and Hartley in his turn held the poet in reverence. He became a convivial favourite with the local country people, who called him 'lile Hartley'. Dorothy described him in 1822 as 'the oddest looking creature you ever saw—not taller than Mr de Quincey—with a beard as black as a raven'; and Harriet Martineau, the writer and social reformer, spoke of his 'wonderfully beautiful conversation'. He died the year before William and the old poet walked over to Grasmere churchyard to indicate the spot where he was to be buried, at the same time marking adjacent plots for himself and Mary.

De Quincey, who had been so much loved by the Wordsworths, was now in disgrace. The relationship had begun to cool earlier, when the stricken parents had found his excessive display of mourning for Catharine tactless and intrusive. Matters had been made worse by what, in William and Dorothy's eyes at least, was a heinous crime. In 1811 Sara Hutchinson wrote to a friend about De Quincey's behaviour at Dove Cottage: 'What do you say to de Q's having polled the Ash Tree and cut down the hedge all round the orchard—every Holly, Heckberry, Hazel, and every twig that screened it . . . all above, and where the Moss hut stood, levelled to the ground.' The final straw was when De Quincey fell in love with a neighbouring dalesman's daughter by whom he had a son. The

RIGHT *Lowther Castle after T. H. Fielding, 1822. Seat of Wordsworth's patron Lord Lonsdale. Wordsworth became increasingly active in political campaigning for the Lonsdale Tory faction, to the dismay of Keats, who had venerated Wordsworth as the apostle of freedom.*

Wordsworths were outraged by the alliance, disapproving of De Quincey's disregard for what was then the accepted barrier between the gentry and the lower classes. Dorothy had written in the early Dove Cottage years of being out in a hail storm:

> Little Peggy Simpson was standing at the door catching the hail stones in her hand. She grows very like her mother. When she is sixteen years old I daresay, that to her grandmother's eye she will seem as like to what her mother was as any rose in her garden is like the rose that grew there years before.

De Quincey's love, this same rose-like Peggy Simpson, was now considered a most unsuitable consort. Dorothy's tone about the pair, who married the following year, was acid:

> Mr de Quincey is married; and I fear I may add he is ruined. By degrees he withdrew himself from all society except that of the Simpsons of the *Nab* . . . At the up-rouzing of the Bats and the Owls he regularly went thither—and the consequence was that Peggy Simpson . . . presented him with a son . . . This is in truth a melancholy story!

In spite of their flouting of convention, the De Quinceys were happy together; but friendship with the Wordsworths was a thing of the past. De Quincey was showing signs of opium addiction, and possibly William and Dorothy felt unable to face another such involvement. De Quincey felt bitter. 'Never describe Wordsworth as equal in pride to Lucifer,' he declared, 'no; but, if you have occasion to write a life of Lucifer, set down that by possibility, in respect to pride, he might be some type of Wordsworth.'

On 28 February 1816 Caroline, Annette Vallon's daughter, was married to Jean-Baptiste Baudouin, but no Wordsworth attended the ceremony, although William did make a marriage settlement upon her. Dorothy had early expressed a desire to

BELOW *Dorothy in old age. Dorothy's long decline was punctuated by flashes of her old self. For a long time she retained her power of writing rapidly, though the results were confused; and she would sometimes recite poetry in a high voice, particularly to William.*

be present and in 1815 the wedding had been postponed for her benefit, indicating how much the Vallons hoped for a paternal representation. Travelling in France during Napoleon's Hundred Days was out of the question, but when Dorothy continued to make difficulties over the journey after peace was restored the couple decided they could wait no longer. A year later Wordsworth's first grandchild, Louise Dorothée, was born.

A new friend of this time was Benjamin Robert Haydon, the painter of historical scenes. He and Wordsworth had met in 1815 and Haydon was immediately attracted to the poet. He planned to include Wordsworth's portrait in his epic picture 'Christ's Entry into Jerusalem', first making a life mask, as he described in his journal:

> I had a cast made yesterday of Wordsworth's face. He bore it like a philosopher. John Scott was to meet him at breakfast, and just as he came in the plaster was put on. Wordsworth was sitting in the other room in my dressing-gown, with his hands folded, sedate, solemn, and still. I stepped in to Scott and told him as curiosity to take a peep, that he might say the first sight he ever had of so great a poet was in this stage towards immortality.
>
> I opened the door slowly, and there he sat innocent and unconscious of our plot, in mysterious stillness and silence.

In December 1817 Haydon made a sketch of Wordsworth's head, while Wordsworth read Milton and his own 'Tintern Abbey'. Haydon recorded his admiration:

> He looked like a spirit of Nature, pure and elementary. His head is like as if it was carved out of a mossy rock, created before the flood! It is grand and broad and persevering. That nose announces a wonder. He sees his road and his object vividly and clearly and intensely . . . In moral grandeur of Soul and extension of scope, he is equal to Milton.

ABOVE *Page from Haydon's sketchbook, to which Keats added his own drawing of the artist, which is labelled 'A vile caricature of B. R. Haydon by Mr. Keats'.*

The previous year the young Keats, Wordsworth's junior by twenty-five years, had written admiringly of the elder poet in his fine sonnet, 'Great Spirits now on Earth are Sojourning':

He of the cloud, the cataract, the lake,
Who on Helvellyn's summit, wide awake,
Catches his freshness from Archangel's wing . . .

He was now eager to meet Wordsworth and this Haydon obligingly arranged. Shortly after their first encounter Haydon gave a party in his studio, where the huge canvas of 'Christ's Entry into Jerusalem', which by now included portraits of both Keats and Wordsworth among the spectators, dominated the scene. He later wrote an account of the occasion:

On 28th December, the immortal dinner came off in my painting-room, with 'Jerusalem' towering up behind us as a background. Wordsworth was in fine cue, and we had a glorious set-to—on Homer, Shakespeare, Milton, and Virgil. Lamb got exceedingly merry, and exquisitely witty; and his fun in the midst of Wordsworth's solemn intonations of oratory was like the sarcasm and wit of the fool in the intervals of Lear's passion. He made a speech and voted me absent, and made them drink my health. 'Now', said Lamb, 'you old lake poet, you rascally poet, why do you call Voltaire dull?' We all defended Wordsworth, and affirmed there was a state of mind when Voltaire would be dull. 'Well,' said Lamb, 'here's Voltaire—the Messiah of the French nation, and a very proper one too.'

He then, in a strain of humour beyond description, abused me for putting Newton's head into my picture; 'a fellow', said he, 'who believed nothing unless it was as clear as the three sides of a triangle'. And then he and Keats agreed he had destroyed all the poetry of the rainbow, by reducing it to the prismatic colours. It was impossible to resist him, and we all drank 'Newton's health, and confusion to mathematics'.

RIGHT *Drawing of John Keats by Benjamin Robert Haydon. Haydon enjoyed Keats's company and arranged for him to meet Wordsworth, whom the young poet greatly admired.*

145

Despite Lamb's light-hearted taunts, for the most part the spirit of the times could still happily accommodate together both arts and sciences. Coleridge, for instance, with his keenly analytic intellect, had been so exhilarated by the inventions of his friend Humphry Davy that he planned to establish a laboratory in Keswick where he and his friends could engage in a course of scientific study. Davy, for his part, found nothing incongruous in pursuing his parallel pleasures of writing poetry and exploring electro-chemistry. And Keats, at the time of Haydon's Christmas party, had completed a long apprenticeship as apothecary surgeon, latterly at Guy's Hospital.

During his walking tour of the Lake District and Scotland in June of the following year, Keats called at Rydal Mount but found no one at home. He wrote a note and propped it on the mantelpiece. He was shocked to learn that Wordsworth, for him the apostle of freedom, was deeply involved in the current election, but on the 'wrong' side: that is, in support of the Tory faction, represented by the Lowthers.

During the next years William worked hard, both on new poems and the revision of old, and in April 1820 his sonnet sequence *The River Duddon* appeared to eulogistic reviews, and was rapidly followed by five more volumes of verse. That year also saw a return to the Alps, where with Mary and Dorothy he retraced his journey of 1790, when he and a friend covered 2,000 miles on foot, carrying their baggage on their heads. On their way home through Paris they met Annette Vallon, Caroline and her husband.

Once back at Rydal Mount the family became involved in rounds of county entertainment, and their social life was extended by more frequent visits to London. William himself remained physically robust, apart from trouble with his eyes, which he now protected with a green shade.

Dorothy spent some months during the winter of 1828 keeping house for her nephew John in his first curacy at Whitwick in Leicestershire. There she was taken desperately ill, with

BELOW *Dora Wordsworth as bridesmaid to Sara Coleridge by Miss Rainbeck, 1829. Dora was the apple of her father's eye. At this time she was an attractive and lively young woman, though worryingly prone to infections.*

what was described as 'internal inflammation'. William was distraught: 'Were She to depart,' he wrote to Crabb Robinson, 'the Phasis of my Moon would be robbed of light to a degree that I have not courage to think of.'

During respites from ill health Dorothy still found plenty to interest her. She wrote of John as giving 'much satisfaction in the pulpit and reading-desk of our little Chapel'. Dora was not well; nevertheless, during a London visit, she was able to enjoy plays and the opera. Her aunt complained of her modish coiffures: 'Yet alas! her poor head has been submitted to a French Hairdresser!—This *does* vex me—I cannot condone the notion of seeing her decked (nay not decked—depressed) by big curls—and Bows and Giraffe Wires.'

In 1830 Dorothy wrote to Mary Lamb that Wordsworth's health continued good: 'He is still the crack skater on Rydal Lake, and, as to climbing of mountains, the hardiest and the youngest are yet hardly a match for him.' She deplored, however, that he still 'shrinks from his great work': this was 'The Recluse', the projected philosophical poem that would continue to elude him until the end.

In the winter of 1817 Wordsworth wrote a letter affectionately recommending Coleridge's lectures to the notice of a friend. 'He talks,' Wordsworth wrote, 'as a bird sings, as if he could not help it: it is his nature.'

Haydon described a later encounter with Coleridge:

> The first person I met after seventeen years was Coleridge, silver-haired! He looked at my bald front, and I at his hair, with mutual looks of sympathy and mutual head-shaking . . . I did not know what to say, nor did he; and then in his chanting way, half-poetical, half-inspired, half-idiotic, he began to console me by trying to prove that the only way for a man of genius to be happy was just to put forth no more power than was sufficient for the purposes of the age in which he lived, as if genius was a power one could fold up like a parasol!

ABOVE *Swiss landscape by Sir George Beaumont. In 1820 Wordsworth returned to the Alps, retracing the footsteps of his youthful journey recorded in* The Prelude. *During this later journey he crossed the St Gothard Pass on foot, returning over the Simplon Pass. The poet was exhilarated by the experience, which he shared with Mary and Dorothy, his fellow travellers.*

ABOVE *Pencil drawing of Whitwick Vicarage by Dora Wordsworth. This was John Wordsworth's first curacy. His aunt Dorothy spent some months housekeeping for him. She approved of his sermons.*

Sara Hutchinson, still a part of the Wordsworth household, paid a visit to Coleridge in 1834 at Highgate, where he had been living since 1816 under the care of Dr Gillman, a young surgeon. She was shocked by his appearance, and the news of his death later that summer was not altogether unexpected. Mary Wordsworth wrote: 'Poor dear Coleridge is gone! He died a most calm and happy death . . . the disease was at his heart.'

The next year, 1835, brought two further sorrows: Sara Hutchinson, who had brought so much gaiety and common sense to the Rydal Mount household, died after an attack of influenza. Dorothy caught the infection and, although she recovered physically, she was left mentally broken, suffering from a form of senile dementia and lingering on in a dim half-light for another twenty years. Strangely, she retained her memory for poems to the end, reciting long pieces in a sweet but plaintive voice: and there were brief periods of lucidity. To Dora she wrote her last letter, sad and incoherent:

My dearest Dora,
They say I must write a letter—and what shall it be? News—news I must seek for news. My own thoughts are a wilderness—'not pierceable by power of any star' . . . Poor Peggy Benson lies in Grasmere Church-yard beside her once beautiful Mother. Fanny Haigh is gone to a better world. My Friend Mrs Rawson has ended her ninety and two years pilgrimage—and *I* have fought and fretted and striven—and am here beside the fire. The Doves behind me at the small window—the laburnum with its naked seed-pods shivers before my window and the pine-trees rock from their base.—More I cannot write so farewell! and may God bless you . . . Yours ever more
Dorothy Wordsworth

William was now at the summit of his renown. Honours accrued to him, including degrees from the universities of Oxford and Durham, a Civil List pension and visits from such

BELOW *Wordsworth, 1839, a be-laurelled portrait of the poet at the height of his fame, aged 69, chosen by himself for Lady Mary Lowther's* Poems and Extracts. *He was made Poet Laureate the following year.*

RIGHT *Coleridge in later life, when living at Highgate with his kind protectors, the Gillmans. He died in 1834. Wordsworth, who acknowledged Coleridge as his chief intellectual influence, and to whom he dedicated* The Prelude, *wrote of his old friend: 'Nor has the rolling year twice measured, / From sign to sign, its steadfast course, / Since every mortal power of Coleridge / Was frozen at its marvellous source; / The rapt One, of the godlike forehead, / The heaven-eyed creature sleeps in earth.'*

notables as Queen Adelaide and her daughter. In 1843, on the death of Southey, he became Poet Laureate. Carlyle described him at about this time:

> Large-boned, lean, but still firm-knit, tall and strong looking when he stood, a right good old steel-grey figure, with rustic simplicity and dignity about him, and a vivacious strength looking through him. He talked with veracity, easy brevity and force, as a wise tradesman would of his tools and workshop . . . His face bore marks of much, not always peaceful, meditation; the look of it not bland or benevolent so much as close, impregnable and hard.

William retained his physical energy, climbing Helvellyn and, in 1841, making a pilgrimage, which he felt to be a final farewell, to the old Somerset haunts of long ago. His delight in his surroundings remained keen. In 1844 he wrote to his publisher Edward Moxon: 'To-day, as I rode up Ullswater side, while the vapours were "curling with unconfirmed intent" on the Mountain sides, and the blue Lake was streaked with silver light, I felt as if no Country could be more beautiful than ours.'

He was delighted with a party given in honour of his seventy-fourth birthday in April 1844: 'I wished you and yours,' he told Moxon,

> could have been with us last Tuesday when upwards of three hundred children, and nearly half as many adults . . . were entertained in the grounds and house of Rydal Mount. The treat went off delightfully with music, choral singing, dancing and chasing each other about, in all directions. Young and old, gentle and simple, mingling in everything.

He continued to enjoy parties, although he tired easily now and would suddenly fall silent. As Poet Laureate he was invited to the Queen's ball in April 1845, borrowing court dress, including

ABOVE *Miss Wordsworth by John Harden, 1842. William often wheeled Dorothy around the garden in her wicker invalid chair. She seemed to enjoy her brother's presence and the fresh air, although the first signs of spring made her weep.*

a bag-wig, from Samuel Rogers, and Humphry Davy's sword. (Less than six years later Rogers would lend the same costume to the succeeding Poet Laureate, Tennyson.) Haydon commented acidly: 'Fancy the High Priest of Mountain and of Flood on his knees in a Court, the quiz of courtiers.'

Ralph Waldo Emerson, the young American poet, visited Rydal Mount towards the end of Wordsworth's life; his encounter with Wordsworth was recorded by Canon Rawnsley, the chronicler of the Lakes:

> he led Emerson out to the terrace path of the garden on which thousands of his lines have been composed, and asking his American visitor if he would like to hear the sonnets on Fingal's Cave, which he had just written, stood forth and gave them with great animation. The recitation was so unlooked for and surprising, the aged Wordsworth standing apart and reciting on the garden walk like a schoolboy declaiming, that it nigh moved Emerson to laughter, but soon won him to listen soberly and attentively enough.

In 1841 Dora married a widower, Edward Quillinan, after a long period of opposition from her father, who could not bear to be present at the wedding. Quillinan, a minor poet and translator, and the father of two daughters, was in no position, his father-in-law considered, to support the increasingly frail Dora. After a long struggle with ill health, Dora died in 1846. Her father was inconsolable, frequently bursting into tears and avoiding all company.

This dearly loved daughter had to a certain extent taken the place of Dorothy during the latter's clouded years. Now, in his grief, William's greatest satisfaction came from attending on Dorothy again, wheeling her around the garden on fine days. Brother and sister were happier when together—Dorothy's illness made her fretful and difficult to please, but William could soothe her. She recited to him and sometimes there were little

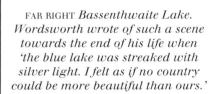

RIGHT *Wordsworth on Helvellyn, 1842, a detail of the magisterial portrait by Benjamin Robert Haydon. Haydon had described him at an earlier sitting as looking 'like a spirit of Nature, pure and elementary'.*

FAR RIGHT *Bassenthwaite Lake. Wordsworth wrote of such a scene towards the end of his life when 'the blue lake was streaked with silver light. I felt as if no country could be more beautiful than ours.'*

flashes of rationality when they could enjoy one another's company once more. Looking back to the rapturous days at Dove Cottage, when they had been everything to one another, when the poet's genius burned the more brightly for his sister's generous outpouring of spiritual strength and loving insight, the image of the old man in the green eyeshade bending over Dorothy's helpless form makes a poignant contrast. It is better to let the mind return to William's lovely blessing from the 'Lucy' poem of long ago:

> *The stars of midnight shall be dear*
> *To her; and she shall lean her ear*
> *In many a secret place*
> *Where rivulets dance their wayward round,*
> *And beauty born of murmuring sound*
> *Shall pass into her face.*

For the next short years William's life continued in its accustomed rhythm. On 10 and 12 March 1850 he walked considerable distances in a cold wind and two days later he developed pleurisy. On 7 April, his eightieth birthday, he was still alarmingly weak; and for a brief space Dorothy, aware of his condition and seeming miraculously to recover something of her old self, visited his room. On 23 April, with all the sounds of a Lakeland spring floating in at the windows, and as the cuckoo clock in his room told midday, Wordsworth died.

Dorothy lived on for another five years, nursed by the saintly Mary. Mary, having witnessed the publication of *The Prelude*, died peacefully of old age in 1859.

Matthew Arnold wrote in his memorial verses:

> *Keep fresh the grass upon his grave,*
> *O Rotha, with thy living wave!*
> *Sing him thy best! for few or none*
> *Hears thy voice right, now he is gone.*

ABOVE *Portrait of Mary Wordsworth by Margaret Gillies, watercolour on ivory, c. 1839. Kind, wise Mary cared selflessly for William and their family, and in particular for Dorothy during the long years of her illness. She outlived both William and Dorothy, and died in 1859, having named* The Prelude *and seen it published. She was 'the solitary lingerer' of those who had carved their initials on the Rock of Names so long before.*

But the final words are Wordsworth's own, as he declared his
faith in the immortality of poets in the last of *The River Duddon*
sonnets, sonorous and valedictory:

> *Still glides the Stream, and shall for ever glide;*
> *The Form remains, the Function never dies;*
> *While we, the brave, the mighty, and the wise,*
> *We Men, who in our morn of youth defied*
> *The elements, must vanish;—be it so!*
> *Enough, if something from our hands have power*
> *To live, and act, and serve the future hour;*
> *And if, as toward the silent tomb we go,*
> *Through love, through hope, and faith's transcendent dower,*
> *We feel that we are greater than we know.*

BELOW *Wordsworth's grave in
Grasmere churchyard. The poet
died on 23 April 1850. On first
seeing Grasmere as a schoolboy he
had thought: 'What happy fortune
were it here to live! / And if I
thought of dying, if a thought / Of
mortal separation could come in /
With paradise before me,
here to die.'*

IN THE FOOTSTEPS OF WORDSWORTH IN THE LAKES

William Wordsworth was born in 1770 in a handsome eighteenth-century house in Main Street, Cockermouth (Wordsworth House), now the property of the National Trust. This is open to the public, is furnished in the style of the poet's time, and contains a Wordsworth museum. Behind the house the terrace looks on to the River Derwent. At Hawkshead Grammar School, Wordsworth's desk, carved with his name, is still on view.

In 1789 William and Dorothy went to live at Dove Cottage on the banks of the lake at Grasmere. The little house, now owned by The Wordsworth Trust and open to the public, has been carefully restored—one of its rooms for example, is lined with newspaper as in Dorothy's own early decoration. The garden climbs steeply behind the house and still gives a feeling of seclusion and space. A summer-house stands on the site of the original moss hut where brother and sister loved to sit. The Wordsworth Museum, close by Dove Cottage, contains fine portraits of the poet and his family and members of his circle, notably Charles and Mary Lamb, and other memorabilia of the poet such as his skates and green eyeshade, together with letters and other documents relating to his life. The nearby library houses the Wordsworth archive.

There is a Wordsworth memorial in Grasmere Church, and the poet's grave is in the churchyard, surrounded by those of his immediate family, and that of Hartley Coleridge. Wordsworth himself planted some of the yew trees.

The mountains in the Lake District are the highest in England, and appear even higher than they are because they rise so abruptly from the valleys. The landscape has altered in some places, water levels have changed, roads constructed, but in the main a short climb brings the walker into a timeless world, where the prospect to be enjoyed is the same as that of the Wordsworths and their friends nearly two hundred years ago. All around lie the places hallowed by Wordsworth's poems and Dorothy's journal: Easedale Tarn; Helm Crag; the much-loved Lancrigg; Grasmere and its island, to which Wordsworth liked to row; the site of Brothers Wood to the north-east end of the lake;

Butterlip How, a favourite viewpoint; Loughrigg Fell; White Moss quarry, where the Wordsworth's encountered the carman and his family; Glow-worm Rock; Bainriggs Wood; John's Grove, where their sailor brother used to pace up and down in solitude, and Grisedale Tarn, where he said goodbye to his brother and sister for the last time, and hurried off down the stony hillside and away.

On Thirlmere's east bank is the site of the Rock of Names, where William, Dorothy, John, Mary and Sara Hutchinson and Coleridge carved their initials. The rock itself was destroyed during road blasting. Over Grasmere and Thirlmere towers Helvellyn, the mountain climbed many times by the poet, for whom it held a profound significance.

The river Rothay links Grasmere to Rydal Water, and high above the eastern end of the lake stands Rydal Mount, Wordsworth's home from 1813 until the end of his life. Containing Wordsworth family mementoes, it is now owned by one of his descendants and is open to the public.

Greta Hall, Coleridge's home from 1800 to 1803 and Robert Southey's from 1803 until the end of his life, is now part of Keswick School. The setting is the dramatic landscape that so enraptured Coleridge, including Skiddaw, the mountain rising to the north of Keswick.

The way down from Kirkstone Pass towards Patterdale taken by the Wordsworths led past Brothers Water, scene of Dorothy's Good Friday walk in April 1802, when she left William sitting on the bridge composing his poem 'The Cock is Crowing'. Wordsworth loved the beauty of Patterdale, passing through it on his way to see John Marshall at Hallsteads, the Lonsdales at Lowther Castle or his Quaker friend Thomas Wilkinson near Penrith. On the west shore of Ullswater, between Stybarrow Crag and Glencoyne Beck, and before reaching Gowbarrow Park and Aira Force, is the bay on the verges of which William and Dorothy saw the daffodils 'Fluttering and dancing in the breeze'. Stybarrow Crag was probably also the scene of the young poet's stealing a skiff, described by him in *The Prelude*.

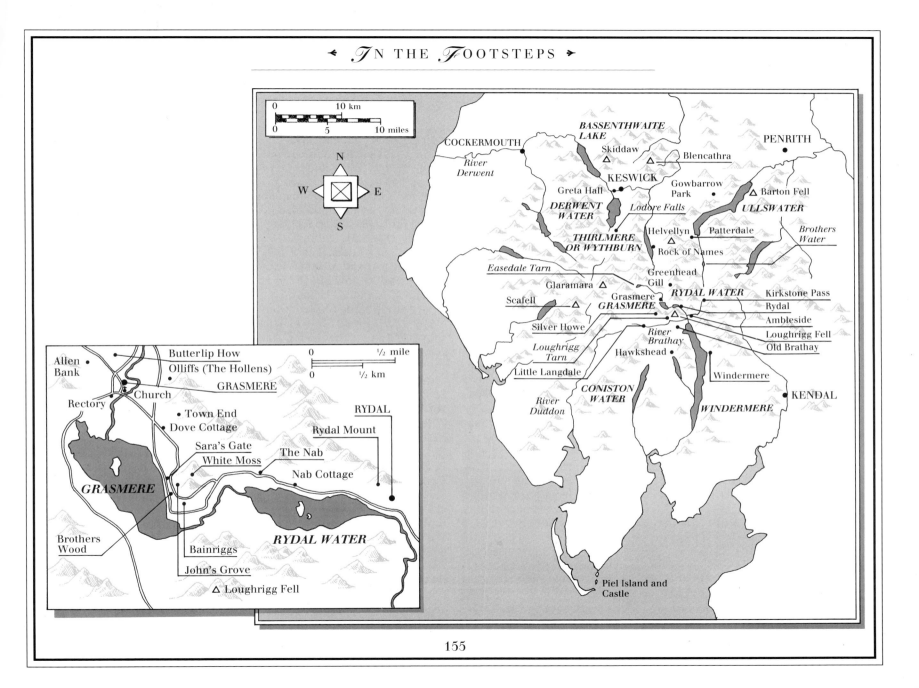

0   10 km
0   5   10 miles

N
W ⊠ E
S

COCKERMOUTH

River Derwent

BASSENTHWAITE LAKE
Skiddaw △
△ Blencathra

PENRITH

KESWICK

Greta Hall

Gowbarrow Park
△ Barton Fell

DERWENT WATER

Lodore Falls

ULLSWATER

THIRLMERE OR WYTHBURN
△

Helvellyn
Rock of Names

Patterdale

Brothers Water

Easedale Tarn

Greenhead Gill

Glaramara △

Grasmere

RYDAL WATER

Kirkstone Pass
Rydal

Scafell △

GRASMERE
△

Ambleside
Loughrigg Fell
Old Brathay

Silver Howe

River Brathay

Loughrigg Tarn

Hawkshead

Windermere

Little Langdale

CONISTON WATER

River Duddon

WINDERMERE

KENDAL

Piel Island and Castle

0   ½ mile
0   ½ km

Allen Bank •
Butterlip How
Olliffs (The Hollens)

GRASMERE

Rectory
Church

• Town End
• Dove Cottage

RYDAL

Sara's Gate
White Moss
The Nab

Rydal Mount

Nab Cottage

GRASMERE

RYDAL WATER

Brothers Wood

Bainriggs

John's Grove

△ Loughrigg Fell

FAMILY AND FRIENDS

BEAUMONT, Sir George (1753–1827), landscape painter and patron of the arts, benefactor of Wordsworth, Coleridge and Haydon. He was an admirer of Wordsworth's poetry and before he had met the poet presented him with a piece of land on which to build a house. Later he lent the Wordsworths a farmhouse at Coleorton on his Leicestershire estate for some months. Beaumont's painting 'Peele Castle in a Storm' inspired Wordsworth to write 'Elegiac Stanzas' in memory of his brother John, drowned off Weymouth Bay.

COLERIDGE, Hartley (1796–1849), eldest son of Samuel Taylor Coleridge. He showed brilliant promise as a child, with a precocious grasp of philosophical concepts. After his father left his wife and family, Hartley was largely brought up by his uncle, Robert Southey. Wordsworth also took an affectionate interest in the boy and arranged for him to go up to Merton College, Oxford. Hartley obtained a Fellowship at Oriel College, but his drunken habits resulted in expulsion. He taught in various schools near Ambleside, and wrote essays and poetry. Physically he was tiny and awkward, with bright black eyes and a black beard. He became increasingly eccentric but continued to inspire affection in the people of the Lake District, making his home at The Nab, Rydal. He is buried in Grasmere churchyard, near the Wordsworths' graves, in a plot selected by Wordsworth.

COLERIDGE, Samuel Taylor (1771–1834), poet, philosopher, metaphysician and critic, famed for his verbal brilliance. In 1794 he first met Southey, later marrying Sara Fricker, Southey's sister-in-law, and settling in Somerset. In June 1797, on a walking tour in Dorset, Coleridge met Wordsworth and his sister Dorothy, and one of the most momentous of literary friendships was immediately under way. During the next year, stimulated by collaboration with Wordsworth, he wrote his most important poems, including 'Frost at Midnight', 'This Lime-Tree Bower my Prison', 'Kubla Khan' and 'The Rime of the Ancient Mariner'. In 1799 the Wordsworths moved to the Lake District, and Coleridge soon followed them, renting Greta Hall near Keswick. Although his marriage had proved a failure, he felt himself bound to his wife and, when he fell in love with Sara Hutchinson (the 'Asra' of his poems), there could be no happy outcome for the pair. He came to depend on opium taken in conjunction with brandy, consequently suffering debilitating illness and depression. His notebooks are the records of his thoughts, emotions and dreams. An unhappy quarrel separated him from Wordsworth, and, although ostensibly patched up, their friendship never fully recovered. His last years were spent in Highgate.

DE QUINCEY, Thomas (1785–1859), prolific writer and critic, author of *Confessions of an English Opium Eater* and one of the liveliest prose stylists of his time. As an Oxford undergraduate he held Wordsworth in veneration, achieving a meeting with the poet and his family in 1807. The Wordsworths were attracted to the young man and, after they left Dove Cottage, De Quincey occupied it for some years. His *Recollections of the Lakes and the Lake Poets*, with its quizzical humour, provides an invaluable picture of the Wordsworths and their circle. De Quincey married Margaret Simpson, daughter of a yeoman farmer, by whom he had eight children. He had begun to take opium while at Oxford and by 1812 he was addicted to the habit. To support his family he turned to journalism, writing mostly in Edinburgh for *Blackwood's* and *Tait's* magazines.

HAYDON, Benjamin Robert (1786–1840), painter of historical subjects on a gigantic scale, best remembered for his portraits and his *Autobiography*, which gives a vivid anecdotal account of literary and artistic London of the era. He met Wordsworth in 1815 and included the poet's portrait in his monumental 'Christ's Entry into Jerusalem'. Haydon's difficult nature militated against his success and finally, overcome with debts, hurt pride and disappointment at his failure to realize his artistic ambitions, he shot himself in his studio.

HAZLITT, William (1778–1830), political and literary critic, and essayist of strongly held liberal views. He first met Wordsworth in Somerset in 1798 and felt, when hearing the poet reading his verse, 'something of the effect that arises from the turning up of the fresh soil, or of the first welcome breath of spring'. In 1803 he visited Keswick and painted portraits of Wordsworth and Coleridge. A scandal, possibly over a dalesman's daughter, forced him to fly precipitately from the Lakes. His essay, 'My First Acquaintance with Poets', contains memorable descriptions of Wordsworth and Coleridge.

HUTCHINSON, family. Like the Wordsworths, the Hutchinsons were orphaned when young. Mary (1770–1859), the eldest girl, attended for a time the same dame school as William Wordsworth. She and Dorothy Wordsworth first became friends when both were living with relations in Penrith. Later Mary and her sisters Sara (1775–1835) and Joanna (1780–1841) kept house for their farmer brothers George and Tom in County Durham and in Yorkshire. Sara Hutchinson and Coleridge met and fell in love in 1799, when the poet visited the family at Sockburn on Tees, Coleridge writing poems to her as 'Asra'. Wordsworth and Mary were married in 1802. Sara, who remained single, made her home for many years with the Wordsworths.

KEATS, John (1795–1821), poet. The son of a livery stable manager, he was early apprenticed to an apothecary-surgeon and later became a student at Guy's Hospital. He abandoned medicine to concentrate on writing poetry. He first met Wordsworth, to whom he had already addressed a sonnet, in 1817. They were both guests at the 'immortal dinner' given by Haydon at the end of the year. After listening to Keats reciting his 'Hymn to Pan', Wordsworth is said to have commented dismissively: 'a very pretty piece of Paganism'. 1818 saw the beginning of Keats's *annus mirabilis*, during which he wrote, among other poems, 'Ode to a Nightingale', 'To Autumn' and 'Ode on a Grecian Urn'.

LAMB, Charles (1775–1834), essayist, writer and wit, best remembered for his *Essays of Elia* and, in conjunction with his sister Mary, *Tales from Shakespeare*. He was educated at Christ's Hospital and there met Coleridge, with whom he formed a lasting friendship. Coleridge's 'This Lime-tree Bower My Prison' was addressed to Lamb, in commiseration with his friend after Mary Lamb had killed her mother in a fit of madness. Wordsworth respected his judgement and sought his comments on his poems (though he did not always act upon these).

ROBINSON, Henry Crabb (1775–1867), barrister, chiefly remembered for his journals and letters containing detailed accounts of his huge circle of acquaintance, including Wordsworth, Coleridge, Lamb and Hazlitt; also Goethe and Schiller. He first met Wordsworth in London in 1808, visited him on several occasions in the Lake District and toured with him on the Continent. He was active in effecting a reconciliation between Wordsworth and Coleridge after their estrangement.

SOUTHEY, Robert (1774–1843), poet, historian and essayist. He and Coleridge in their youth planned a Utopian way of life (Pantisocracy), which, however, was never realized. The two men married sisters, Elizabeth and Sara Fricker. In 1803 he moved to the Lake District, sharing Greta Hall at Keswick with Coleridge and his family. After Coleridge abandoned his wife and children, Southey undertook their care, treating them with generosity and kindness. He and Wordsworth held one another in respect but were never intimates, although on two occasions of distress it was to Southey that Wordsworth first turned for comfort. In 1813 Southey reluctantly became Poet Laureate.

VALLON, Annette (1766–1841), daughter of a surgeon at Blois. She and Wordsworth met in Orléans in 1791 and became lovers. Their daughter Caroline was born in 1792. The war between France and England separated the pair, and William did not see his daughter until she was nine. William met her and Annette on two later occasions. Caroline married Jean-Baptiste Baudouin in 1816.

WORDSWORTH, brothers of William and Dorothy: Richard (1768–1816) was a lawyer. **Christopher** (1774–1846) entered the Church, became Master of Trinity College, Cambridge, and was twice Vice-Chancellor of that university. **John** (1772–1805) was employed by the East India Company, became captain of one of their largest trading vessels and was drowned when his ship sank off Weymouth Bay.

WORDSWORTH, children of William and Mary: John (1803–75) went into the Church and became a country parson. **Dora** (1804–47) married the poet Edward Quillinan and died young. **Thomas** (1806–12) and **Catharine** (1808–12) both died in childhood. **William** (1810–83) succeeded his father as Distributor of Stamps.

INDEX

SOURCES AND ACKNOWLEDGEMENTS

I would particularly wish to acknowledge my indebtedness in the preparation of this book to Stephen Gill's masterly *William Wordsworth: a Life* (1989), complemented by Mary Moorman's earlier two-volume *William Wordsworth: a Biography* (1957 and 1965), which have proved invaluable to me. I have particularly profited from reading David McCracken's *Wordsworth and the Lake District: A Guide to the Poems and Their Places*, and, among the gigantic corpus of modern Romantic studies, Richard Holmes's *Coleridge: Early Visions* (1989), A. S. Byatt's *Unruly Times: Wordsworth and Coleridge in their Time* (1989), Robert Woof's *The Wordsworth Circle* (1979) and Rupert Christiansen's *Romantic Affinities: Portrait of an Age* (1988).

I am most grateful to Robert Woof for all his generous help throughout, and for so kindly reading my manuscript. Elizabeth Drury has been the best of editors, and I am greatly in her debt. Philippa Lewis's picture research has produced extremely beautiful results; Colin Ziegler has been most helpful. I would like to thank the staff of the London Library for their help, and James Hughes-Hallett and Lucy Hughes-Hallett for their encouragement and for detailed and constructive advice.

The illustrations are reproduced by kind permission of the following: Abbot Hall Art Gallery, Cumbria 37, 55, 68, 69, 83, 105, 115 (Bridgeman Art Library), 117, 135, 138, 140/1, 142, 149, 152; Ashmolean Museum, Oxford 75; Bridgeman Art Library 34, 107, 117; Bristol Central Library 110; British Library 15, 30, 33, 57, 79, 113, 127, 129, 142, 151; Christie's Colour Library 39, 123, 139; A.C. Cooper 86; Derby Museum & Art Gallery 51 (Bridgeman Art Library); Fine Art Photographs 31, 66; Leicester Museum & Art Gallery 103, 147; The Mansell Collection 21, 124, 132, 134, 136; National Library of Scotland 84, 85, 87, 104; National Portrait Gallery 16, 17, 20, 92, 111, 130, 132, 140, 144, 145, 150; Rydal Mount, Grasmere 109, 146; Victoria & Albert Museum 23 (Bridgeman Art Library), 24, 40, 52/3, 61, 88/9; The Wordsworth Trust, Dove Cottage, Grasmere 2, 7, 11, 18, 19, 25, 27, 29, 32, 34, 35, 36, 43, 44, 45, 46, 47, 60, 78, 80, 91, 93, 95, 96, 97, 99, 106, 112/13, 114, 122, 126, 128, 134, 137, 147; Yale Center for British Art, Paul Mellon Collection 6, 67.

These illustrations come from the following books:
R. Ayton & W. Daniell, *A Voyage Round Great Britain* (1814–1825): 72; J. & J. Boydell, *A History of the River Thames* (1796): 71; John Curtis, *British Entomology* (1823–1840): 62, 98; E. Donovan, *Natural History of British Birds* (1799–1819): 64, 70, 102; T.H. Fielding, *Cumberland, Westmorland & Lancashire* (1822): 15, 79, 129, 142; C. & T.H. Fielding, *Picturesque Illustrations of the River Wye* (1821): 131; W. Green, *Seventy-eight Studies from Nature* (1809): 33, 42, 113; W. Green, *Sixty Studies from Nature* (1810): 48, 49, 54, 57, 60; T.H. Horne, *The Lakes of Lancashire, Westmorland and Cumberland* (1816): 12, 81, 101; P.H. de Loutherbourg, *Romantic and Picturesque Scenery of England and Wales* (1805): 119; A.C. Pugin, *Microcosm of London* (1808): 73; I.O. Westwood, *British Butterflies* (1841): 63.